Alexander the Great

THE WORLD'S GREAT EXPLORERS

Alexander the Great

By Maureen Ash

CHILDRENS PRESS®

CHICAGO

Marble head of Alexander the Great as the god Heracles

Project Editor: Ann Heinrichs
Designer: Lindaanne Donohoe
Cover Art: Steven Gaston Dobson
Engraver: Liberty Photoengraving

**Library of Congress
Cataloging-in-Publication Data**
Ash, Maureen
  Alexander the Great / by Maureen Ash
    p.   cm. — (The World's great explorers)
  Includes bibliographical references and index.
  Summary: Traces the life of the warrior king
of Macedonia who conquered and united the
known world of his time.
  ISBN 0-516-03063-9
  1. Alexander, the Great, 356-323 B.C.—
Juvenile literature. 2. Greece—History—
Macedonian Expansion, 359-323 B.C.—Juvenile
literature. 3. Generals—Greece—Biography—
Juvenile literature. 4. Greece—Kings and
rulers—Biography—Juvenile literature. [1.
Alexander, the Great, 356-323 B.C. 2. Kings,
queens, rulers, etc. 3. Generals. 4. Greece—
History—Macedonian Expansion, 359-323 B.C.]
I. Title. II. Series.
DF234.A84 1991   91-13862
938'.07'092—dc20   CIP
[B]   AC

Scene on Alexander's coffin, showing a battle between Greeks and Persians; in the Archaeological Museum of Istanbul, Turkey

Table of Contents

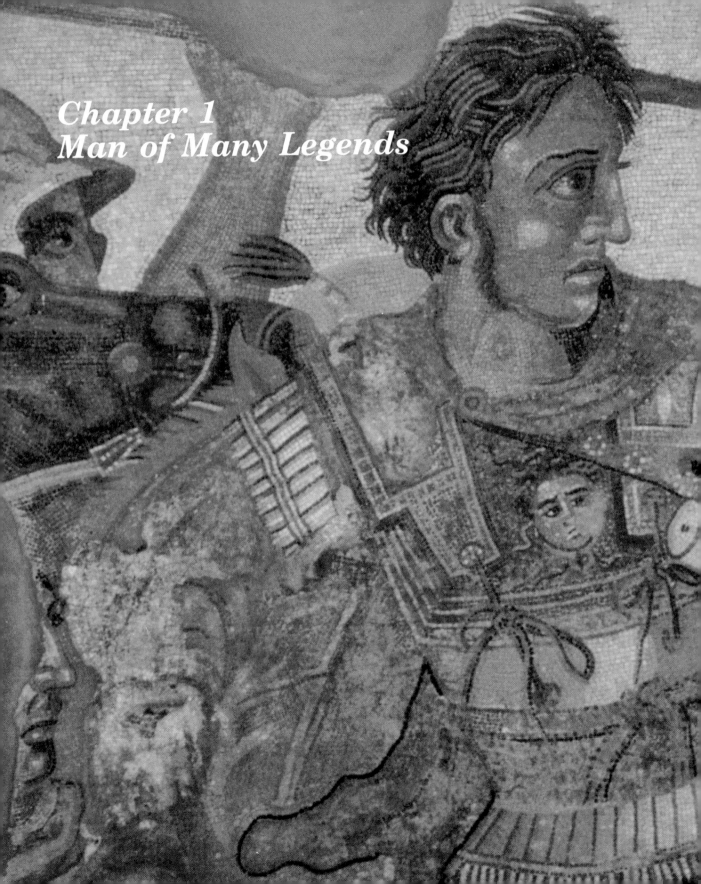

Chapter 1
Man of Many Legends

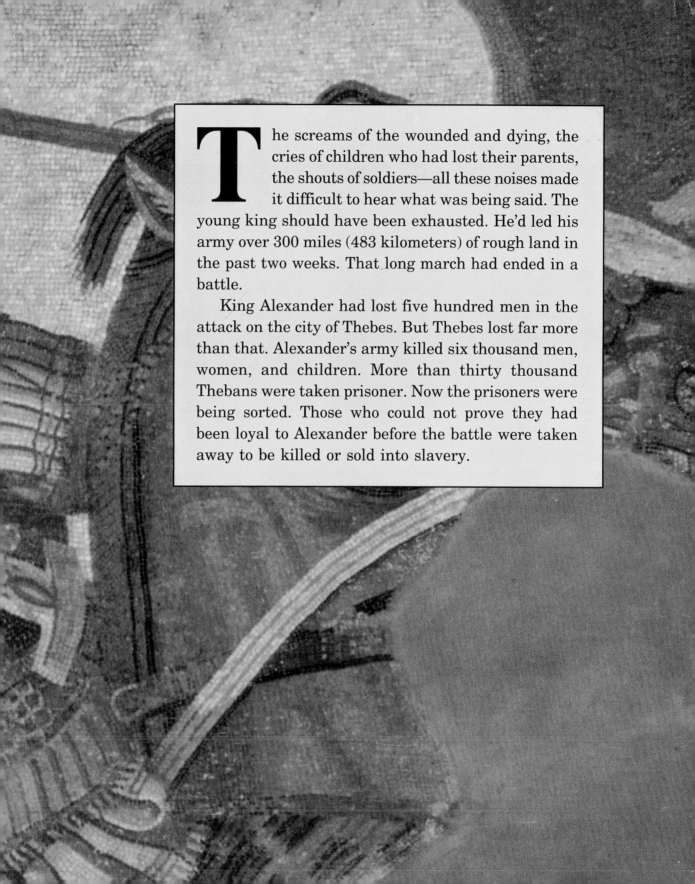

The screams of the wounded and dying, the cries of children who had lost their parents, the shouts of soldiers—all these noises made it difficult to hear what was being said. The young king should have been exhausted. He'd led his army over 300 miles (483 kilometers) of rough land in the past two weeks. That long march had ended in a battle.

King Alexander had lost five hundred men in the attack on the city of Thebes. But Thebes lost far more than that. Alexander's army killed six thousand men, women, and children. More than thirty thousand Thebans were taken prisoner. Now the prisoners were being sorted. Those who could not prove they had been loyal to Alexander before the battle were taken away to be killed or sold into slavery.

The Theban prisoners were in shock. Their city had been invaded, their families killed. They faced either death or life as slaves in unknown lands. They waited, huddled and miserable, to learn what lay ahead for them.

Alexander looked out among them and noticed a woman who did not look frightened. She stood with her head up and held her children to her side.

Alexander had her brought to him. She had murdered one of his officers, his men told him. The woman did not deny this. She told Alexander how the man had broken into her house and looted it. She had tricked him into believing her jewelry was hidden in a well. Then, when he'd leaned over to look for it, she pushed him in and dropped stones on him until he was dead.

The courageous Theban woman throwing one of Alexander's officers into a well

The woman was not sorry for what she had done to protect her home and children. Alexander asked her who she was. He learned that she was the sister of the man who had led the Thebans against Philip, Alexander's father, in another battle. She was not sorry for that, either. She stood tall, waiting to die.

Alexander watched her. He understood and admired her loyalty to her home, family, and city.

"She will not die," he said. "And she will not be a slave. Let her go." He ordered some soldiers to help the woman and her children to a safer place.

After this act of kindness, Alexander returned to sorting prisoners like cattle. Then he ordered that the city of Thebes, except for its temples and the house of Pindar, a poet, be destroyed. Court musicians played as buildings were looted, wrecked, and burned.

Theban woman confronting Alexander the Great

Pindar playing his lyre as he sings his poetry

This is just one of the stories about Alexander that has lived through the ages. No one can be sure how much of it is true. His army did destroy Thebes, except for the temples and Pindar's house. Thousands of Thebans were killed and the rest sold into slavery. Did Alexander spare the life of one brave woman and her children?

We don't know. For every known fact about Alexander, there seem to be two or three legends. Because there are so many, and because they have lasted so long, the stories tell us that Alexander must have been more than a military genius or a gifted

ruler. His personality must have been electrifying. He led an army of thirty thousand men from Greece into India. Men more than twice his age fought battles and crossed mountains and deserts because Alexander was their leader. They loved and trusted him.

Alexander lived only thirty-three years, but he and his army conquered much of the world that was known to them. In addition to this, Alexander encouraged the exchange of ideas between the various people he ruled. He changed the world as it was known two thousand years ago. Even today it is hard to understand how one man could have done so much.

Alexander the Great was a man of many legends. This drawing of Alexander receiving a gift of elephants is from a fifteenth-century French story of his life.

Chapter 2
Alexander: His Father's Child

Greece is a small, mountainous country on the Balkan Peninsula. This piece of land extends down from eastern Europe into the Mediterranean Sea between Italy and Turkey. Greece's soil is poor, its rainfall is light, and yet for thousands of years people have raised grain, olives, grapes, and other fruits there. Greek products are used throughout the world today, and modern-day Greece is growing more and more influential.

Greece's true age of glory, however, was more than two thousand years ago. Art, music, literature, and drama flourished there. Public architecture was so beautiful that people have used it as a model of perfection ever since.

These things are important, certainly. But other empires had grown before, some more magnificent than the Greek civilization. Their leaders had concentrated, however, on achieving wealth and power. The Greek civilization was based on individual freedom. Greece became the birthplace of democracy, or government by the people. Of all the ideas, art treasures, and writings left to us by that ancient civilization, the concept of a government based on individual freedom is the most important. This is one of the ideas Alexander the Great spread across the nearly one million square miles (2.6 million square kilometers) of his empire.

If you compare a map of the world today to a map of the world the Greeks knew in 356 B.C., you begin to understand how little the people then knew about the earth. Only the Mediterranean Sea and the Italian and Greek peninsulas are in any sort of proportion. Europe is squeezed down to almost nothing, and the Iberian peninsula, occupied now by Spain and Portugal, is shown to be the same size as Italy. The great continent of Africa takes up only a small space and is called Libya. And Persia and India, the lands shown to the east of the Mediterranean, cover the areas we now call Iraq, Iran, Afghanistan, Pakistan, and India. Nothing was known then of the rest of the continent we still call Asia. Alexander and his teachers did not begin to guess at the millions of square miles that lay to the north and west of them as they studied geography in the palace at Pella, in Macedon.

You won't find a country called Macedon, or Macedonia, on a map of the world today. Now it is just a region that is part of Greece, Yugoslavia, and Bulgaria. We remember Macedon now for what it was

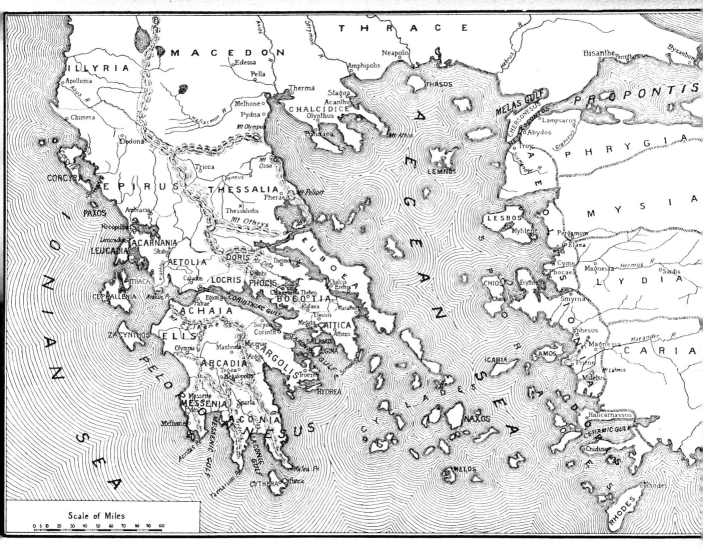

Ancient Greece and its colonies

more than two thousand years ago. We might not take note of it at all if Alexander the Great had not been born and raised there.

Macedon in 340 B.C. was a kingdom on the northern part of the Balkan Peninsula. The southern part of the peninsula, where Greece is today, was hilly and dry. In places, there were fertile valleys where settlements had grown into cities. Each city, along with its surrounding territory, was known as a *polis*, or city-state. Each had its own government and laws and army.

15

A classic sculptor at work on a statue of the Greek god Zeus, known to Romans as Jupiter

The Greek city-states could have worked together to form a common government and a larger, better army. That way they could have shared natural resources and protected their trade routes better. The peninsula would have been more difficult for other armies to invade. Instead, the city-states fought each other, which made them weak.

Philip II, king of Macedon and Alexander's father, noticed this. He spent part of his youth in the Greek city-state of Thebes as a hostage. It may be that the Thebans felt safer from attack by Macedonians with a member of Macedon's royal family among them. Thebes was a large and powerful city-state. Greek culture—the appreciation of art, science, music, and literature—flourished there. Philip was educated with other Greek boys his age. He must also have paid close attention to the Greek-style military.

Early Greek armor

When he was eighteen years old, Philip was allowed to return to Macedon. It probably looked rough and wild to him after his civilized life in Thebes. Philip's homeland was rugged. In places the mountains started straight up out of the sea. Many Macedonians lived in tribal groups. There were few cities. Philip knew that the citizens of Thebes and other Greek city-states thought that Macedonians were barbarians. He'd probably been taunted when he was in Thebes. The Greeks believed themselves to be the most cultured people in the world. Everyone else was a barbarian.

Philip was a proud, handsome man. He was intelligent and talented at leading men. According to Macedonian tradition, the royalty of Macedon were descended from Greeks. Philip, no doubt, found this easy to believe. After he returned to Macedon, Philip took charge of the army.

A mosaic plaza in Pella, the capital of ancient Macedon

Philip must have spent this time thinking about his kingdom's strengths. Compared to the lands around the Greek city-states, Macedon was very rich. The rough mountains held forests and mines. The Greek city-states built their ships with Macedonian lumber and made their weapons and ornaments with Macedonian metals. Fruit grew on the Macedonian plains, where tribes herded their sheep and cattle and raised fine horses. Macedonians were famous for their horses and horsemanship. So why, he must have wondered, was Macedon such a small, poor kingdom?

A few years later, Philip's father, King Amyntas, died. The crown passed, one after the other, to Philip's two older brothers. Philip, meanwhile, was becoming known as a brilliant military leader. When his brother Perdiccas was killed in battle in 359 B.C., Philip's victories convinced his countrymen that he should be king. They gave him the crown.

Philip married Olympias, the princess of Epirus, in 357 B.C. Epirus, a kingdom to the southwest of Macedon, then became part of the Macedonian empire. Alexander was born a year later, in 356 B.C.

Olympias was beautiful. When she was sixty years old, the story is told, two hundred soldiers were sent to her house to kill her. They broke in, but when they looked at her, they went away without harming her.

Olympias kept tame snakes as part of her religion. She was intelligent and well-spoken, but her jealousy and ambition sometimes made her cruel. She arranged the murders of at least two people in her lifetime. She was unhappy in her marriage to Philip and grew to hate him. In fact, in the end, she may have been behind Philip's murder.

Olympias may have hated Philip, but she loved Alexander. She paid close attention to his education and training. Her greatest ambitions were for her son. Throughout Alexander's career, even when he was far away in Asia, she would write to him with requests and directions. He bore it patiently but was once heard to say that his mother charged a lot of rent for the nine months' lodging she had given him.

You might think that a prince would be free to do as he wished. Alexander, prince of Macedon, was anything but free. His education began early. Leonidas, cousin to Olympias, was chosen to be his tutor.

Leonidas believed that a future warrior should learn to live with hunger and cold and hard exercise. Alexander's childhood was filled with cold swims, long runs, and light meals. Later in life, Alexander said that Leonidas had given him the best cooks: a night march to make him want his breakfast and a small breakfast to make him want his supper. The older man also went through Alexander's belongings frequently to be sure Alexander's mother wasn't slipping her boy any forbidden treats to eat.

The young prince also had to learn to read and write. Most children at that time did not. But Philip was not just creating a Macedonian empire for himself. He was raising a son to be king of it after him. Alexander practiced speaking, for one day he would

The artist Raphael included many of the great Greek philosophers and scientists in this painting, entitled "The School of Athens."

have to inspire his troops for battle. He studied warfare and learned to use a sword and a spear. And like all Macedonian boys who hoped to be warriors, he learned to ride and spent hours every day on horseback.

There are many stories about Alexander as a young boy. One tells of the seven-year-old prince entertaining two Persian governors who arrived at the palace while Philip was away. Alexander is said to have asked them such intelligent questions about their country and its army that they went away amazed.

Greek statue of a musician playing the kithara, a type of lyre

Another story is about Alexander's music lessons. The boy asked his teacher, "Why does it matter if I play one string rather than another?" The teacher replied, "It does not matter—for a future king. But it is very important for a future musician."

Alexander must have decided that it *did* matter which string he played, for there is another story about him at the age of nine. His father was entertaining ambassadors from Athens, one of the most important Greek city-states. After dinner, Alexander was brought in to perform. He played the lyre, recited, and debated with another boy.

At the age of eleven, according to another well-known story, Alexander was watching his father and some other horsemen choose horses for the Macedonian cavalry. One stallion was an especially fine horse but could not be calmed enough to mount. Regretfully Philip waved it away. Alexander exclaimed that a fine animal was being wasted. Philip was probably as delighted to hear this as any father today is glad for his son to tell him that he doesn't know what he is doing. Philip asked Alexander if he thought he could manage the horse. Alexander said that he could. "And if you can't?" asked Philip.

"I'll pay the price of the horse," Alexander vowed. The horse cost thirteen talents, an enormous sum for anyone to pay.

Philip decided to let his son make a fool of himself. It would teach him a lesson. He told Alexander to take the horse. If he failed to manage it, he'd have to pay the thirteen talents. If he succeeded, Philip would buy him the horse.

Alexander walked toward the horse, who reared and plunged, wet with sweat. The boy took the lead rope from the handler and turned the horse to face the sun. The horse immediately became quieter. Before, when the sun was behind the horse, it had been frightened of its own shadow. Alexander let the horse catch its breath, then leaped onto its back. The horse galloped away, the boy clinging to its back. Before long, young Alexander turned the animal and cantered it back to his father, who must have been as proud as he was amazed. According to legend, Philip said, "You must find a kingdom worthy of yourself, my son. Macedon is too small for you."

Alexander named the horse Bucephalus, which means ox head, because the black stallion had a white mark shaped like an ox head between its eyes. Bucephalus carried Alexander into battle for the next eighteen years. When the mighty horse died, Alexander founded a city and named it Bucephala, to honor his faithful companion.

These are all stories about the young Alexander, and there are more. They might be true, or partly true. Or they might just be stories. One fact we know about Alexander is that Aristotle, one of the most famous philosophers in history, became Alexander's tutor when the prince was thirteen years old.

Aristotle, philosopher of ancient Greece

Alexander with his beloved horse Bucephalus

Philip had chosen boys of royal blood to be Alexander's companions. They were called royal pages. They were sons of leaders of some of the Greek city-states and of kings of lands Philip had conquered. They were held partly as hostages, as Philip had been in Thebes. But Philip must have hoped that Alexander would find friends among them and thus prevent future conflicts with neighboring lands. Aristotle was summoned to teach Alexander and the royal pages.

The Trojan horse, presented as a gift but filled with warriors, enabled the Greeks to win the Trojan War.

The poet Homer, author of the epic poems Iliad and Odyssey

No one knows what they studied, though Aristotle is believed to have written two books for his young charges. Looking back at Alexander's life and the interest he had in natural science, medicine, and philosophy, we can guess that Aristotle schooled Alexander in all of these.

The boys also studied the *Iliad*, a long poem that describes the Trojan War. This war was fought long before Alexander's time. As the *Iliad* recounts, the princes of ancient Greece set out to rescue the wife of Menelaus, king of Sparta. She was Helen, the most beautiful woman in the world, and she'd been taken away by Paris, the prince of Troy. The war lasted ten years. The poet Homer, who wrote the *Iliad*, emphasized the courage and nobility of the warriors. One of

Achilles, the legendary hero of the Trojan War, could only be wounded in one spot—his heel. Thus, our term "Achilles' heel" means a special weakness that can cause someone's downfall.

the Greek heroes who fought was Achilles. He was brave, skilled at fighting, clever, and thoughtful.

Alexander believed that Achilles was one of his ancestors. At first the young prince hoped to be like Achilles. Later, he hoped to achieve more than Achilles had. He memorized most of the *Iliad* and kept a copy of it under his pillow at night (as well as a dagger) wherever he went for the rest of his life.

Aristotle widened Alexander's view of the world. At the same time, the older man insisted that non-Greeks had no worth except as slaves. Alexander had met and known people from many different cultures. He'd seen that there were strengths and weaknesses in all ways of living. He continued to judge people on their merits and not on their ancestry.

As Alexander grew up, his father conquered new lands for Macedon. In twenty years of fighting and diplomacy, Philip was able to double the size of his kingdom.

Philip had a talent for leading men in battle. He also had a talent for preparing men to fight. Few armies before Philip's had practiced fighting, but Philip trained his men all year round. They were strong and seasoned. He also changed the way they fought.

The Greeks fought mostly on foot, with spears and shields. They were organized into a unit called a phalanx—a formation of soldiers eight rows deep. When the army attacked, the phalanx marched forward, thrusting spears into the enemy. When the phalanx was attacked, the men formed a square, with spears pointing out.

Philip used the phalanx in his army, but he made their shields wider and their spears much longer. Now the phalanx marched forward, strong and square. To keep the enemy from slipping around it, Philip added wings of archers, foot soldiers with light weapons, and armed men on horses.

As Philip conquered more kingdoms and countries, he gained more treasure, horses, and men to fight for him. He began to dream of conquering all the Greek city-states. Then, as that dream began to seem a reality, Philip thought about invading Asia and conquering the rich Persian empire.

Philip knew that to be successful in Asia, he would need all of Greece and the surrounding areas united behind him. He spent years preparing for the great invasion of Asia by conquering or forming alliances with the Greek city-states and the lands to the north and east of Macedon.

Philip was away for two years, battling for control of Thrace, a region east of Macedon. Alexander, aged sixteen, remained at the palace in Pella. His father had appointed him regent, or acting king.

Alexander had his first test in battle when he led Macedonian troops against a rebellious neighboring tribe. It was his first recorded victory, and it must have felt wonderful. He'd trained all his life to fight men in battle.

The young prince must have sent news of his first military victory off to his father with more than a little pride.

We'll never know whether Philip felt proud of his son, but some records show that he probably did. He returned to Macedon when Alexander was eighteen and put his son in charge of the cavalry in a great battle against Thebes and Athens. The Macedonian army was victorious.

Philip made a mistake as he prepared for his great invasion of Asia, and it had nothing to do with his military plans. He fell in love with a young Macedonian woman and took her as one of his wives.

This frightened Olympias, Alexander's mother, and Alexander, too. If Cleopatra, Philip's new wife, had a baby boy, Philip might decide that the boy was his heir. The baby would grow up to be king, not Alexander.

Alexander, of course, didn't want this to happen. And Olympias wanted her own son to be king. She refused to attend the wedding feast.

Alexander attended the wedding, however, and there was exotic food served on golden dishes as dancers in beautiful costumes entertained the guests. Wine flowed freely.

Girls dancing in an ancient Greek bas relief

It was probably too much wine that prompted Attalus, the new bride's uncle, to call out, asking the gods to give Cleopatra a son. This son, he said, would be of pure Macedonian blood and therefore the rightful heir to the throne.

Alexander got angry and quarreled with Philip. The king rose from his chair as if to strike Alexander, but he'd had too much to drink and he fell over. The stories tell us that Alexander said, "See there, the man who wishes to cross into Asia. He falls crossing from one chair to the other." The angry young man stalked away and left Macedon with his mother.

Philip and Alexander made up, but Alexander was still nervous about his future. When they quarreled again, Philip punished Alexander by sending some of his best friends away to other countries. They were not allowed back to Macedon. Alexander, now twenty years old, must have hated being under his father's heels. Nevertheless, he did as he was told. He, too, wanted to conquer the Persian empire.

Through battling and making treaties and alliances, Philip persuaded the Greek city-states to form the League of Corinth. This was an association of the city-states, kingdoms, and tribes of Greece. Under the League's treaty with Philip, he would not interfere with the affairs of the individual governments. He only required that the members of the League back him in his foreign policy. Philip announced his aims: to free the cities that Greeks had settled in Asia and to take revenge on the Persians for their attack on Greece over a hundred years earlier. The Greeks hated the Persians and appointed Philip to lead the new, united Greek army against them. Philip was at last ready to march into Asia.

Then he was murdered.

He was murdered by one of his bodyguards, a man named Pausanias. Rumors flew, but most evidence points to Olympias, his wife, as the one behind the plot to kill the king.

One thing is certain. Philip had been a great general. He had set the stage for Alexander's later triumphs. Philip's highly trained army, his military strategy, and the League of Corinth were important to Alexander's early success.

Pausanias murders Philip II.

Chapter 3
Subduing the Grecian States

Alexander honored the memory of his father with an elaborate funeral. But his thoughts were on how to keep control of the lands and people his father had conquered. Other men wanted to be king, but Alexander quickly had these men killed. A king had to be cold and hard, and Alexander began to prove that he was both.

When the regions Philip had conquered learned that Philip was dead, some began to revolt. Alexander quickly showed them that he had the same control of his father's army that his father had had. He defeated rebellious troops in Thessaly, the region just south of Macedon, then marched farther south to Corinth. There the League agreed that Alexander should be general of the Greek forces, as his father had been. He was twenty years old.

Alexander meeting with Diogenes, a wise and peculiar man

One story about Alexander takes place in Corinth. The philosopher Diogenes lived there. Diogenes lived very simply. Sometimes he wore a barrel instead of clothing. Once he walked through the city at night with a lantern, searching for one honest man. Alexander wanted to meet such an interesting person. When he went to see him, Alexander found the philosopher sitting on the ground thinking. His shadow fell over Diogenes, who remained seated. Alexander, after introducing himself, offered to grant Diogenes a request. Diogenes requested that Alexander step aside and stop blocking the sun. The young king did so, laughing good-naturedly. "Were I not Alexander," he said, "I would wish to be Diogenes."

Once, while Alexander and his companions were still studying with Aristotle, the old philosopher asked the boys what they would do in a certain situation. Each student answered. When it was Alexander's turn to respond, he said that he'd wait until it happened and then he'd see.

That may have been the answer Aristotle was looking for. At any rate, Alexander's willingness to be flexible in different situations had a great deal to do with his success.

We see this first in his battle against a group of Thracians. They held a mountaintop and planned to defend it by rolling heavy wagons down onto any advancing soldiers. It was a clever scheme. The mountain was rough and could be climbed only through its narrow passes. The wagons were poised over the passes.

Alexander sized up the situation. He ordered his men to attack. If the Thracians roll the wagons down, he told the men, lie down under your shields.

The men did as they were told. After the wagons had rumbled over them, the men got up and continued up the mountain. The Thracians quickly surrendered. Alexander's men must have marveled at the cleverness of their young commander.

They would marvel again. Perhaps after a while it began to seem normal for Alexander to think of new ways to solve old problems.

After defeating the Thracians, Alexander thought it would be wise to conquer the tribes far to the north of Macedon. To do so, he would have to cross the Ister River, which we know today as the Danube. Neither he nor any of his men had ever seen such a wide, swift river before.

The superior Greek army defeats the Thracians

The Getae, the tribe on the other side of the river, felt safe from attack. They were wrong. Alexander ordered his men's tents, which were made of animal hides, to be stuffed with hay. The tents were used as rafts that night, and four thousand foot soldiers and fifteen hundred cavalrymen and their horses crossed the river.

Once on the other side, the foot soldiers marched through tall grass. They flattened it for the cavalry by holding their long spears, called sarissas, sideways as they marched.

Greek warriors preparing for battle

The Getae panicked and ran. Alexander's men plundered their town and took women and children as captives, to be sold as slaves. Alexander sacrificed to the gods, thanking them that none of his men had drowned. Other tribes in the area heard about what had happened to the Getae. To avoid the same fate, they came and paid tribute to Alexander.

From the Ister River, Alexander marched to Illyria, north of Epirus, roughly where the country of Albania is today. After he put down an uprising there, he learned that there was trouble in the south.

The Thebans, urged on by the city-state of Athens, had made a treaty with Persia. The allies swore to oppose Alexander or any other Macedonian king. In fact, because there had been so little news of the army, there was a rumor that Alexander was dead.

The king of Macedon marched his army through well over 100 miles (161 kilometers) of mountain passes in six days. He arrived in central Greece, picked up more troops, and made it to the gates of Thebes in another six days. These swift marches were to become one of Alexander's trademarks.

He sent messengers to the leaders of Thebes, offering to accept their surrender and to hear their terms. They did not agree to surrender, so Alexander's army

The site of Thebes

overran the city. Alexander is said to have spared the life of the Theban woman who killed one of his officers. But he ordered the city to be destroyed, except for the temples and Pindar's house. He'd made an example of Thebes, and he might have felt some guilt about it. Records show that for the rest of his life Alexander tended to help Thebans wherever he found them because he had destroyed their home.

News of what had happened to Thebes traveled fast. The people of Athens and other city-states were horrified. Athenians sent a group of their leaders to congratulate Alexander on his northern victories and to ask for peace. Alexander accepted. Now, with Greece united behind him, he was ready to invade Persia.

Scene in ancient Athens

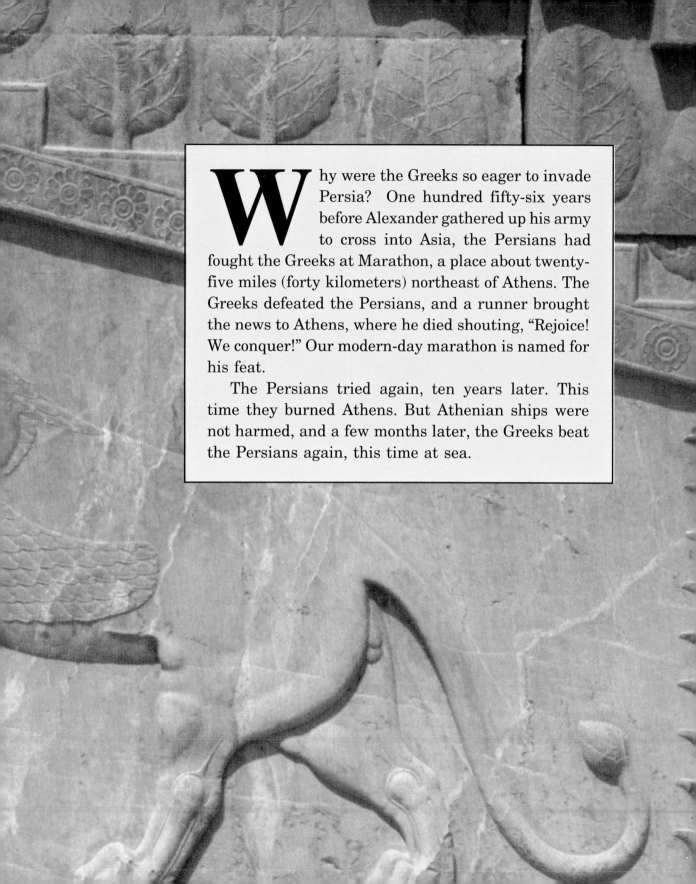

Why were the Greeks so eager to invade Persia? One hundred fifty-six years before Alexander gathered up his army to cross into Asia, the Persians had fought the Greeks at Marathon, a place about twenty-five miles (forty kilometers) northeast of Athens. The Greeks defeated the Persians, and a runner brought the news to Athens, where he died shouting, "Rejoice! We conquer!" Our modern-day marathon is named for his feat.

The Persians tried again, ten years later. This time they burned Athens. But Athenian ships were not harmed, and a few months later, the Greeks beat the Persians again, this time at sea.

Sixty years later, the Persians attacked again. Now they took possession of the island of Cyprus and the Greek cities in Asia. The Greeks, naturally, hated the Persians for this. When Philip, Alexander's father, proposed invading Asia, he tied the invasion to the Greek dream of revenge on the Persians. His private objective was, no doubt, to be ruler of the Persian empire. But the objectives he stated to the League of Corinth were what every Greek desired: revenge on the Persians and freedom of the Greek cities on the Asian continent. These cities along the east coast of the Mediterranean Sea and had been settled by Greeks but taken over by Persians.

The Persian empire itself stretched across Asia to India, north to the Caspian Sea, and south to Egypt. This, remember, is just about as much of Asia as Alexander knew existed. The Persian king, Darius III, was rich and commanded a huge army, far bigger than Alexander's.

Maybe Alexander himself wondered how his army would ever defeat the Persians. There is a story about Alexander visiting the oracle at Delphi, a city northwest of Athens, before he left for Asia.

An oracle is a priest or priestess who was believed to receive hidden knowledge from a god. A person seeking an answer to a question or wanting to know what the future held would present the question to the oracle. The god would then reveal an answer, speaking through the priest or priestess.

Alexander, naturally, wanted to learn from the god what was in store for him. The priestess at Delphi told Alexander that the god, Apollo, could not be approached that day. Alexander, who was not a patient man, dragged her by her hair to the altar.

The priestess at Delphi

"My son," she told him, "you are invincible." Whether this was her prophecy or simply her own opinion, Alexander was satisfied. He began the march toward Persia.

The Hellespont is the narrow channel between the Aegean Sea, which washes Greece's eastern coast, and the Black Sea, within the ancient Persian empire. The Hellespont separates Europe from Asia. Today we call it the Dardanelles. Alexander and his army crossed the channel in boats, the king in the lead. When he was near enough, Alexander cast his spear to the Asian shore as an omen—he would conquer it by force. He was first to wade ashore.

Achilles, hero of the Trojan War, dragging the body of Hector, his defeated foe

He marched first to Troy, to honor Achilles, his hero from the *Iliad*'s story of the Trojan War. Then he turned and led the army to the river Granicus, where part of the Persian army waited for them.

Alexander's armor shone, and he sat proudly on Bucephalus. He wore two white plumes on his helmet. He led the charge up the riverbank and battled his way toward a Persian leader he saw. He killed the man with his spear, took a blow on his helmet, and would have been sliced by another Persian's scimitar if Cleitus, the brother of his childhood nurse, had not cut off that soldier's arm.

The Persians eventually fell back and ran away. The Greeks had won their first victory against the Persians.

Alexander's victory at the Granicus River

Alexander gave special funerals to his men who had died in battle. He declared that their families would not longer have to pay taxes, and he had their statues cast in bronze. He visited his wounded soldiers, asking how they'd been wounded and encouraging them to talk and brag about their deeds.

Alexander also buried the Persian generals with honors. And he released without punishment the local people who had been forced to fight for the Persians.

The next cities were easy to conquer. They were the Greek cities the Persians had taken years before, and the citizens were glad to have a Greek ruler again. Alexander was fair to the cities that surrendered to him. He restored democracy and removed leaders who had been unjust.

He had to fight for the city of Miletus. Its leader had been ready to surrender but then learned that Darius, the Persian king, had sent four hundred warships to defend the city. Somehow Alexander learned this, too, and slipped his own one hundred sixty ships into the harbor first.

Darius III, king of Persia

Alexander's highest ranking general, Parmenio, urged a sea battle because the Greeks had a better position. But Alexander said that he did not want to risk the skill and courage of his soldiers and sailors. He knew the Persian ships were manned by more experienced seamen. In addition to this, the Macedonian soldiers had seen an eagle perched on shore, ahead of their ships. To Alexander, this meant he should attack by land.

His ships closed the harbor to Persian ships, then he launched his land attack. The city fell. The battle had given Alexander an idea.

Map showing the routes of Persian invasions of Greece and the Greek cities in Asia Minor (now Turkey). Miletus is at the lower right.

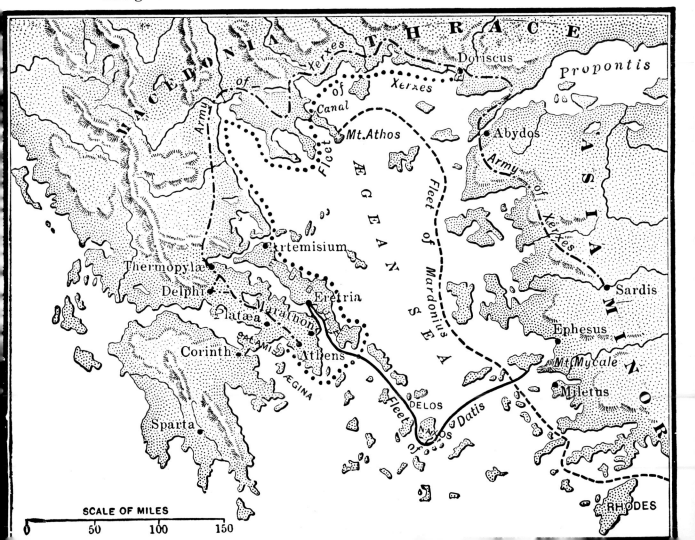

SCALE OF MILES
50   100   150

The Persian Empire often relied on ships for military conquests. The Persian fleet was wrecked (above) while battling the Greeks in 480 B.C. near the Greek island of Salamis.

Warships at that time carried seamen, who navigated and sailed the ship; rowers, who provided the power to move the ship; and soldiers, who fought in battles against enemy troops on shore or on another ship. So many men required a huge amount of water and supplies. A warship almost always sailed with supporting land troops, who gathered supplies for the ships. Alexander noticed that the four hundred Persian ships had sailed without supporting troops.

So Alexander sent soldiers to occupy the coast and keep the Persian vessels from landing. With no supplies coming in, the ships soon had to leave. Alexander

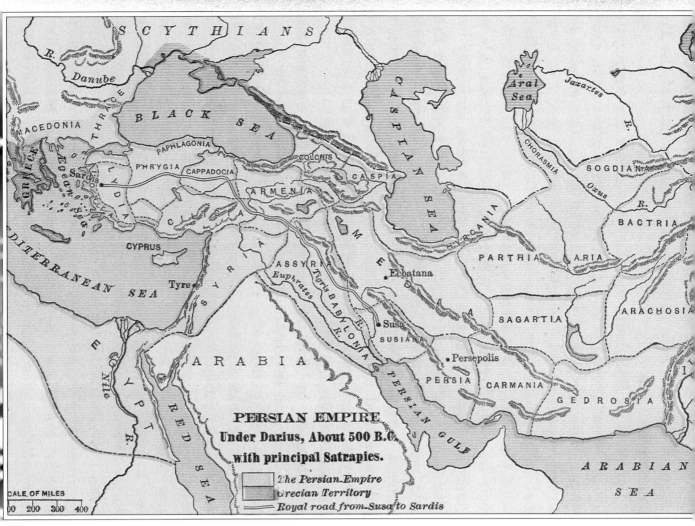

PERSIAN EMPIRE
Under Darius, About 500 B.C.
with principal Satrapies.

The Persian Empire
Grecian Territory
Royal road from Susa to Sardis

SCALE OF MILES
0 200 300 400

decided to conquer the whole Persian fleet by capturing every city on the eastern Mediterranean seaboard. With no place to land for supplies, the Persian ships would be useless.

Alexander captured several more cities before winter. Then he granted home leave to soldiers who had married before the army left for Persia. This made him even more popular and beloved by his men. Those who remained with him helped him fight the hill tribes, who had moved down into the valleys for the winter. Then they moved down the coast, attacking cities as they went along.

This map shows how far the Persian Empire extended in 500 B.C. under Darius I the Great. Darius III, who reigned in Alexander's time, was the great-great-great-great grandson of Darius I.

47

By spring, Alexander was at Gordium, near present-day Ankara, Turkey. This city was famous for its Gordian knot. The knot was a made of a strip of cornel bark. The bark was wound around the yoke and pole of a wagon that was said to have carried the famous King Midas. (The long spears, or sarissas, carried by Macedonian foot soldiers were also carved from sturdy cornel wood.) Whoever untied the Gordian knot, the legend said, would rule Asia. It seemed to Alexander that the knot had been waiting for him.

Ruins of the city of Gordium, Turkey, with the burial mound of King Midas in the background

There are two different stories of how he bested the Gordian knot. One says that he worked the yoke off the pole and exposed the inside of the knot, where the loose ends were. Untying the knot was easy from there. The other story is that he simply drew his sword and cut through the knot. The stories fit the personality of Alexander—he was both clever and impatient. At any rate, one of his historians wrote, "There were thunderclaps and flashes of lightning that very night."

Alexander getting ready to cut the Gordian knot

Chapter 5
Darius, Issus, and the
Siege of Tyre

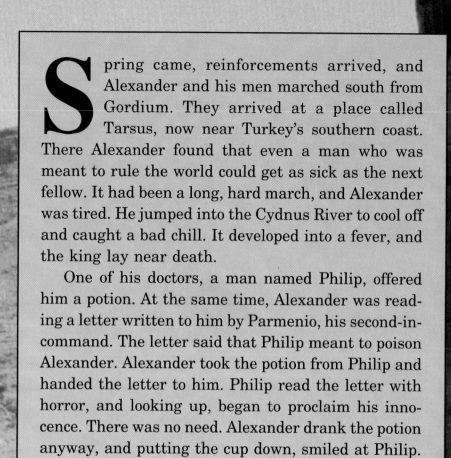

Spring came, reinforcements arrived, and Alexander and his men marched south from Gordium. They arrived at a place called Tarsus, now near Turkey's southern coast. There Alexander found that even a man who was meant to rule the world could get as sick as the next fellow. It had been a long, hard march, and Alexander was tired. He jumped into the Cydnus River to cool off and caught a bad chill. It developed into a fever, and the king lay near death.

One of his doctors, a man named Philip, offered him a potion. At the same time, Alexander was reading a letter written to him by Parmenio, his second-in-command. The letter said that Philip meant to poison Alexander. Alexander took the potion from Philip and handed the letter to him. Philip read the letter with horror, and looking up, began to proclaim his innocence. There was no need. Alexander drank the potion anyway, and putting the cup down, smiled at Philip. The young king knew that Philip was his friend. Alexander risked his life to prove his faith in Philip's loyalty. And his faith was well founded. He got better.

Alexander takes the potion offered him by his physician, Philip, in spite of a rumor of Philip's plan to poison him.

Alexander was sick for two months, though, and in that time the Persian emperor Darius had marched west to meet him. Darius's army was huge—sixty thousand or more. Still, Alexander and his men were eager to engage the Persians in battle. They marched 80 miles (129 kilometers) in less than forty-eight hours. And while they marched, Darius and the Persian army were on the move, too. The two great armies passed each other at night, a mountain range between them.

Darius and his men arrived in Issus, near the border shared by today's Turkey and Syria, expecting to meet Alexander soon. Instead, they found sick and wounded Macedonian soldiers in a field hospital that Alexander had set up. The Persians cut the hands off

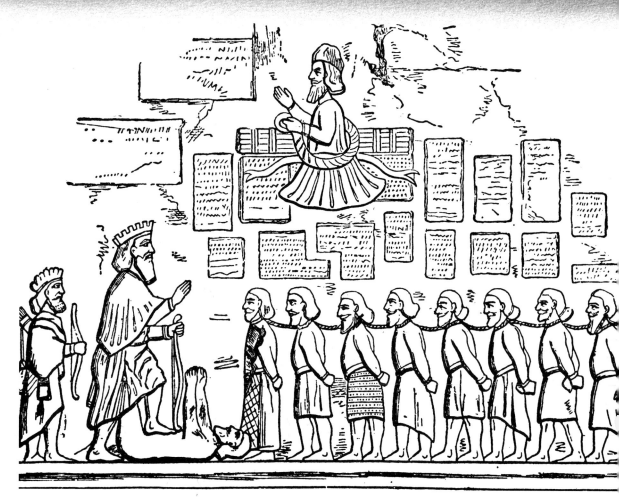

Rock carving of Darius dealing with captured people after one of his conquests

the Macedonian soldiers. Some of the people of Issus were so repelled by this cruelty that they raced to tell Alexander.

Alexander was crossing Pillar of Jonah pass in the Taurus Mountains of southern Turkey when he heard the news that Darius was behind him. He ordered his weary soldiers to turn around. They would meet Darius on the narrow coastal plain between the mountains and the sea.

When the two armies met, each side fought furiously. Alexander, on Bucephalus, led the cavalry and smashed through the Persian line. He had his eye on Darius, who was six-and-a-half feet (two meters) tall, standing in a beautiful chariot and wearing a royal robe.

Alexander (left) and Darius (right of center) at the Battle of Issus

Darius saw Alexander heading for him and turned his chariot. He fled for his life, leaving his soldiers in a panic. They raced to get away from the Macedonian army, and here the narrow battlefield squeezed between the mountains and the sea worked to Alexander's benefit. Thousands of Persian soldiers had waited in the rear, ready to come in as reinforcements because there was not room for them on the narrow plain. In their mad retreat, the Persian soldiers trampled many of the reinforcements.

Alexander and his men chased the Persian king but could not catch him. Darius had even abandoned his mother, wife, and daughters. After the battle, when Alexander entered the Persian's royal tent and saw the table laid for the Persian king's dinner, with bowls and pitchers of solid gold, he said, the story goes, "This, it would seem, is to be a king."

"Alexander the Great with the Women of Darius," a painting by Giovanni Battista Tiepolo

In Alexander's time, captured women were considered spoils of war—property that the victors might seize. Alexander, however, treated the women of Darius's family with kindness and courtesy. He ordered that they continue to receive the care and respect they were used to having, though it meant they would be treated better than he himself.

After visiting his wounded soldiers and congratulating those he had seen performing acts of bravery, Alexander and his best friend, Hephaestion, went to visit Darius's mother and wife. Hephaestion entered the tent first, and the queen mother knelt before him, thinking he was Alexander. When she realized her mistake, she became frightened of what the real king would do to punish her. Alexander, according to the stories, merely smiled. "Never mind," he said. "He too is Alexander."

Alexander and the queen mother became friends—such friends, in fact, that ten years later she is said to have starved herself to death, mourning Alexander's passing.

Darius, meanwhile, was regrouping his army in Mesopotamia, a Greek word meaning "between rivers." The region lay between the Tigris and Euphrates rivers, in what is now Iraq, to the southeast of Alexander's troops in Issus. From Mesopotamia, Darius wrote to Alexander asking what ransom the Macedonian wanted for the royal Persian family.

Alexander answered Darius that the royal family would be restored to him when the Persian leader came to ask for them in person.

"And in the future when you send to me, send to the lord of Asia," wrote Alexander; "and do not write to me what to do, but ask me, as master of all you own, for anything you need. Or I shall judge you an offender. If you claim your kingdom, take your stand and fight for it, and do not run, for I shall make my way wherever you may be."

Alexander wanted to march into Mesopotamia to pursue Darius. However, he saw that it would be more practical to first cut off the Persian navy by capturing the empire's major port cities.

One of the most important of these was Tyre, a city on the Mediterranean Sea in what is now southern Lebanon. Tyre was built on an island in the sea and surrounded by high walls. It could not be attacked from land or by ship. Alexander would have to think of something else.

Alexander had learned about the natural sciences and medicine from his tutor Aristotle. The king continued to be interested in those things. As he traveled

The peninsula of the city of Tyre. The fortified island became a peninsula after Alexander placed stones between it and the mainland.

into and across Asia with his army, he also brought with him a group of botanists, astronomers, other scientists, and historians. From his father, Alexander had learned the importance of engineers in making war. Alexander employed a corps of engineers skilled in the art of building machines and structures that would enable the army to enter a walled city.

At Tyre, Alexander's engineers had their skills taxed. The king wanted them to build a causeway, or road, across a half mile (.8 kilometer) of ocean.

Everything had to be done by hand or horse. There was a staggering amount of earth and rock to be moved, and the wheelbarrow had not been invented yet. As the causeway was built, the engineers designed new, improved siege towers. Fully assembled, these towers were 180 feet (55 meters) tall. For easier transport, the engineers made them collapsible. There were platforms at the top where archers could stand and shoot arrows down into the city. Lower down, there were platforms for men and battering rams to work at breaking the wall. The towers' timbers were coated with lime to make them more resistant to fire. Animal hides were hung to protect the soldiers on the tower from arrows and spears. Alexander also had his

Catapults designed by Greek military engineers

engineers build stone-tipped poles mounted on wheels. These would be rolled to the wall and used to drill through it.

The engineers had already designed catapults that shot several arrows at once, catapults that threw stones, and portable drawbridges. Those machines, and siege towers built earlier, were part of the reason the army had been so successful already.

At first, construction of the causeway went well enough. But as soon as the workers were within range of the city, the Tyrians pelted them with missiles from their own catapults. Then they sent a burning ship adrift to float into and burn the towers Alexander was building.

Greek siege machines in action

Plutarch, who wrote biographies of great people of ancient Greece and Rome

Alexander ordered that new towers be built. And he set off to find more ships for his fleet.

He brought his old friend, the elderly Lysimachus, along for company. They were scouting the hills one day when Alexander once again proved what a loyal friend he could be. The historian Plutarch wrote:

"But when, leaving their horses, they began to walk into the hills, the rest of the soldiers went a good way ahead, so that night approaching and the enemy near, Alexander lingered behind so long, to hearten and help the lagging tired old man, that before he knew it he was left in the rear a long way from his soldiers, with a small company, on a bitter night in the dark, and in a very bad place; till seeing many scattered fires of the enemy some way off, and trust-

Ancient Phoenician sailors were known as great mariners.

ing to his swiftness . . . he ran straight to one of the nearest fires, and killing with his dagger two of the barbarians who sat by it, snatched up a burning brand, and returned with it to his own people. They at once made a great fire, which so scared the enemy that most of them fled, and those that attacked them were soon routed; and thus they rested securely for what was left of the night."

Soon after this, Alexander arrived in Sidon, near Tyre, where 120 ships from Cyprus were waiting for him. The island had been Greek once, and its rulers wished it to be so again. With the ships and sailors and soldiers were engineers from Cyprus and Phoenicia (now Lebanon), who joined the Greek engineers in designing ever-better siege towers.

Seacoast between Tyre and Sidon

Alexander mounted catapults on his ships and rowed them in to blast the walls of Tyre with stones. The Tyrians dropped huge boulders into the sea, making it difficult to maneuver the ships close enough to the walls to shoot the catapults. Alexander had the boulders fished up and thrown away. To do this, the ships would have to drop anchor. The Tyrians knew this and sent armored ships to cut the anchor cables. Alexander sent more ships. Then the Tyrians used underwater divers to cut the cables. Next, Alexander switched from using cable to using chain.

As the causeway drew closer, the Tyrians grew more inventive. They heated sand red hot and shot it from their catapults onto the Macedonians. The histo-

Today's port of Tyre, Lebanon

rian Diodorus wrote, "It sifted down under their corselets and their clothes, searing the flesh with intense heat . . . they screamed entreaties like men under torture, and none could help them, but with the excruciating pain they went mad and died."

The causeway was not yet complete when Alexander planned the final attack. He used siege towers mounted on ships to breach the walls. Once inside, the Macedonian soldiers were relentless. They killed mercilessly, and the historian Arrian wrote that they took thirty thousand people as captives to be enslaved. The causeway was never removed. To this day the city of Tyre, for centuries an island, stands on the end of a small peninsula.

While building the causeway, Alexander had had another offer of terms from Darius. The Persian leader offered Alexander ten thousand talents for his family, as well as an enormous amount of land, a treaty of alliance, and the hand of his daughter in marriage.

Alexander's general, Parmenio, said, "I would take it, were I Alexander." Alexander replied, "I too, were I Parmenio." He wrote to Darius that he had no need of money and that he would not take as a gift land that he already held. He would marry the Persian's daughter if and when he pleased, and if Darius wanted an alliance, he should come and ask for it.

The siege of Tyre took between seven and nine months. The army was probably glad to be marching on, this time to Egypt. But between them and Egypt lay Gaza. It was built high on a steep mound and was thought to be impregnable. Alexander didn't like to

Alexander at the siege of Tyre

think anything was impossible, but he did not attack Gaza simply for the challenge of it. He didn't want to leave a strong Persian city in his rear—Darius could use it against him.

Once again Alexander called for his engineers. They must have walked around the base of the mound, discussing what to do. Finally they decided to build a second mound, so high that they could drag their catapults up and fire down into the city.

The work was somehow accomplished in less than two months. In the battle to take the city, Alexander was wounded twice, once in the thigh by a dagger and once by a catapulted arrow, which had the force to pierce his breastplate and enter his shoulder. The chest wound was serious, but he recovered. Now he was free to march into the richest, most mysterious part of the Persian empire: Egypt.

Alabaster sphinx in Memphis, Egypt, where Alexander was enthroned as pharaoh

Chapter 6
From Egypt to the
Persian Capital

In Egypt, Alexander was welcomed as a hero and deliverer. His soldiers, many of whom had never even seen Athens, the largest city in Greece, were awed by the temples, pyramids, and enormous statues. They followed the rich river Nile to Memphis, where Alexander was enthroned as pharaoh. In the eyes of the Egyptians, Alexander was truly a god.

In Memphis, Alexander sacrificed to the Egyptian gods, which pleased the Egyptian priests, who had great power over the people. He also held games there for athletes and performers from Greece.

The Pharos, or lighthouse, of Alexandria was built in the third century B.C. during the reign of Ptolemy II, son of Alexander's general Ptolemy I. Ptolemy I founded Alexandria's famous library and museum, and Ptolemy II made the city the center of Greek learning. The lighthouse stood on a small, rocky island in the harbor of Alexandria and was destroyed by earthquake in the 1200s. Pharology, the study of lighthouse construction, took its name from the Pharos.

During the winter, Alexander sailed to the mouth of the Nile. West of the river's mouth, he noticed a site that seemed excellent for a city. He stopped and enthusiastically showed the men with him where the temples and meeting places should be. He used grain to map out the street patterns, and birds flew down to eat it. He was afraid that this was a bad omen, but his seers assured him it meant that the city would be prosperous and feed many people. He named the city Alexandria, and it thrives even today.

After marking out his city, Alexander was, Arrian wrote, "seized with a longing to visit Ammon in Siwah." Siwah was an oasis in the desert, west of where Alexandria was to be. There a famous oracle lived, the oracle of the god Ammon. Alexander may have decided to visit Siwah because the legendary heroes Perseus and Heracles had done it. Perhaps he wanted to know what lay ahead as he continued his conquests. At any rate, it was a difficult journey through the arid desert of western Egypt. Dust storms could come up that might engulf an elephant. The king and his companions ran short of water. Legend says that Alexander was guided by two talking snakes.

Alexander on his conquest of Egypt

Alexander visiting the oracle of Ammon at Siwah

At Siwah, Alexander visited the oracle. No one ever leaned what it was that he asked, but it is recorded that the pharaoh and king was well satisfied with the answer he got. The rumor was that Alexander had been told he was the son of a god. Certainly from then on he seemed to feel that he was.

Alexander left Egypt in the spring of 331 B.C. He marched back to Tyre, where he made sacrifices and held more games. From there he turned east. It was time to meet Darius again.

From mid-July until mid-September, Alexander's army marched north and east. As the soldiers marched, Alexander passed the time by hunting, administering the affairs of his growing empire, and overseeing the army.

By all accounts, Alexander loved physical challenges. Hunting was, for him, a pleasant, active, and often exciting way to relax and take his mind off his other duties. Managing his empire took a great deal of time and thought, and it probably wasn't the sort of activity he enjoyed. Governing then (and now) involved the reading and writing of many letters, the settling of disputes large and small, the collection of taxes, and the distribution of tax money.

Managing his army, on the other hand, seems to have been a pleasure for Alexander. He loved being loved by his men. He made every effort to make their lives more comfortable and less dangerous. He knew thousands of them by name. He never asked anyone to do anything he would not do, and he rewarded any act above and beyond the call of duty, whether it was bravery in battle or a willingness to carry a heavier load.

Alexander's men were fiercely loyal. They followed him across rivers, deserts, and steep mountain ranges.

Sophocles, a Greek playwright and poet who lived from 496 to 406 B.C. He wrote more than 120 plays, but only seven of them have survived.

In addition to his other duties, Alexander found time to read. He had nearly memorized his beloved *Iliad*, but he also read history and modern poetry. Later in the campaign, he would be happy to receive the plays of Sophocles, a great Greek poet and playwright.

Certainly as his army drew nearer to the Mesopotamian city of Babylon, where Darius was waiting, Alexander hunted, read, and worried less about the lands he had already conquered. He had to get his men across the swift Tigris River. He did this by positioning two rows of cavalry across the river. The upstream row of horses broke the current for the crossing infantry, and the downstream row could catch

The Tigris River flowing past Ashur in Iraq

any man swept off his feet by the water. Alexander crossed at the head of the infantry, then stood on the bank to point out the shallow places. The men all crossed safely.

The army camped on the east bank of the Tigris and rested. On September 20 there was an eclipse of the moon. Probably Aristotle had explained the cause of this event to Alexander, but he calmed his panicky men by making sacrifices and explaining that the moon represented Persia. The shadow moving across it was their army.

For the next four days, Alexander allowed his men to rest. Scouts reported on the actions of Darius. Alexander himself rode out to the battlefield.

The Persian leader was not going to repeat the mistake he'd made by meeting Alexander between the mountains and the sea back at Issus. Darius had chosen to meet Alexander on a wide plain near the village of Gaugamela, a few miles from the ancient city of Nineveh, now in northern Iraq. There his huge army would have room to maneuver.

Darius ordered an army of slaves to make the plain even smoother and more level. He planned to use two hundred battle chariots, and they would work best on a smooth surface. The poles of the chariots were fitted with spearheads, and there were blades on the wheels. As the wheels turned, the blades whirled and could cut down men and horses. Darius also ordered that stakes be driven into the ground to stop a cavalry charge. He placed elephants in his front lines—in front of his own chariot, in fact. Horses that have not seen elephants before are terrified of them.

Meanwhile, Alexander talked with his generals, thinking of a battle plan. The generals urged him to attack at night. The Persian army was too big to be taken in any way but surprise, they said. Alexander refused. He said that he would not steal a victory. He knew this would be the most important battle for control of all of Persia. He wanted to defeat Darius once and for all, leaving no question that he, Alexander, was the stronger. Also, he figured that a night attack would create too much confusion. Too many Persian soldiers might break away and form other armies, which would have to be fought another day. No, Alexander told his generals. They would attack by day.

The Persian army was enormous. People who have studied the history of Alexander have different ideas about how large it was. Some say there were 200,000

infantry and 40,000 cavalry. Others say there were more. All agree that Alexander's army of around 40,000 infantry and 6,000 cavalry was very much outnumbered. There was a real risk that, once the fighting started, the Macedonian army would be surrounded. Alexander thought of a plan to combat this. He formed mixed units of cavalry and infantry and positioned them at angles back from the main line of troops. He stationed a reserve line of spear-bearers behind his main troops. If the Persians did try to surround his army, the mixed units and the reserves were to form a rectangle around the regular army. The Persians would be facing a rectangle of bristling spears.

Alexander fighting the battle of Gaugamela. This battle is also called the battle of Arbela (present-day Erbil, Iraq), although it did not take place at Arbela.

The night before the battle, Alexander sacrificed to the deity whose name meant Fear. But when he spoke to his troops the next day, he was calm, confident, and inspiring. They rode to the battlefield and formed up as had been planned.

When the Persian battle chariots charged, the Macedonian soldiers parted, as they had been instructed to do. The chariots were hard to maneuver, and as the vehicles rumbled past, their drivers were killed with spears or arrows.

Alexander led a charge at an angle against the left wing of the Persian army. This enabled the cavalry to avoid the stakes that had been placed to spear their horses. After battling enough to draw more Persian soldiers to that area, Alexander turned his unit and cut back to the center of the Persian line. He had avoided the elephants.

Soon after this, King Darius turned once again and fled for his life. Alexander followed him but turned back to help his army complete the fighting. The dust on the battlefield was so thick that many Persian soldiers didn't realize that their king had gone. The thick dust is probably one good reason we don't know more about this battle. Those who fought in it were probably able to see only what was happening within a few yards of them.

How did the Macedonian army, so small compared to the Persian, win such a great victory? One military historian, E. W. Marsden, wrote that one reason was that the Macedonians had better morale, probably because they felt closer to their commander, Alexander. Another reason was that Alexander had such a detailed understanding of the art of war. Marsden wrote about a third reason:

"It is difficult to re-create the chaos characteristic of full-scale engagements at certain stages, the confusion caused by noise, movement and dust, the atmosphere of doubt and uncertainty, the horrible carnage. . . . It must be extraordinarily difficult for modern generals to remain calm and detached when controlling operations in a command-post some miles from the scene of the fighting. How much harder it would be for Alexander and Darius who were stationed in the line of battle itself! Darius appears not to have possessed that rare ability to sift conflicting reports, to make correct observations, and, remaining cool and unflurried, to issue swift and well-considered orders in such circumstances. Alexander had this ability in a pronounced degree. That was the third decisive factor at Gaugamela."

Drawing of a Persian chariot

Alexander, after the battle was over, raced away again to find Darius. But the Persian was long gone. The Macedonian army moved on, 300 miles (483 kilometers) south to Babylon.

There was no need to storm the ancient city. One of Darius's generals, Mazaeus, who had fought Alexander at Gaugamela, came out to meet the Macedonians and surrender the city to their leader. Alexander entered Babylon in a golden chariot. The road was strewn with flowers, and the priests of Babylon danced a greeting.

Babylon, in existence since the 3000s B.C., was one of the world's first great cities. Its walls were 180 feet (55 meters) thick, made of brick and tar, and enclosed

Alexander's entry into Babylon

The Hanging Gardens of Babylon

60 square miles (155 square kilometers). Crops could be grown within the walls in case of siege. Now Babylon is a ruin about 55 miles (89 kilometers) south of Baghdad, Iraq.

More than two hundred years before Alexander rode through its gates, Babylon had been ruled by a powerful king. Named Nebuchadnezzar, or Nebuchadrezzar, he had a magnificent palace with six hundred rooms. For his wife, Nebuchadnezzar had built the Hanging Gardens of Babylon, a series of manmade terraces planted with cedars and other trees. These gardens were later named as one of the Seven Wonders of the Ancient World.

Cyrus the Great of Persia had conquered the people of Babylon in 539 B.C. Since then, there had been several attempts at revolt, always unsuccessful. As punishment, the Persians melted down the gold statue of the city's supreme god. Temples and shrines were damaged. Darius, a descendant of Cyrus the Great, had filled Nebuchadnezzar's palace with treasures and beautiful furniture.

The treasury of Babylon was impressive, and Alexander was able to give his men rich rewards for their services. He asked that plants from Greece be added to the Hanging Garden's terraces, although only some ivies were able to grow in the hotter climate. Alexander ordered that Babylon's temples be restored.

Instead of ousting Mazaeus, he made him the satrap, or leader, of the city. But he put Macedonians in other important offices. This was his method of ensuring that life in Babylon would go on pretty much as before, but that the city and its leaders would be loyal to him.

Alexander let his men rest and enjoy Babylon for five weeks, then marched east to Susa, in what is now southern Iran.

The leader of Susa also surrendered to Alexander. It was another beautiful city, but what impressed Alexander and his men most was its treasury. It held gold and silver that would be equal to many millions of dollars today.

Alexander loved giving gifts, and now he could do it to his heart's content. His men had so much money now that when they marched, a moving market marched with them. One ancient writer described it this way:

A modern aerial view of Susa

"A moving world was his camp . . . the market that followed him was like a capital city's; anything could be bought there, were it rare as bird's milk."

From Susa, Alexander, his army, and his army's followers marched south and east to Persepolis, the capital of the Persian empire. Today, the ruins of Persepolis are about 30 miles (48 kilometers) northeast of the Iranian city of Shiraz.

On the way to Persepolis, Alexander and his party had to cross the Zagros Mountains, where they were attacked by a local Persian satrap and his forces. Alexander's army had marched into a narrow gorge called the Pass of the Persian Gates.

Ruins in Persepolis, Iran

The Persians had blocked the pass with a wall and began rolling boulders onto the army below. Alexander quickly marched his men out of danger. That night, a local man showed the Macedonians a route around the mountain. Alexander and a small force scrambled around on the narrow, dangerous track and attacked the Persians, taking them by surprise. The main army then broke down the wall blocking the Persian Gates and passed through without trouble.

From the pass, they marched onto a plain of incredible richness and beauty. On the road to the city, according to the historian Diodorus, they met thousands of Greeks who had been slaves of the Persians in Persepolis. They had escaped the growing panic in the capital city. Some were old men who had been slaves for many years. They were hideous to see.

Diodorus explains: "All had been mutilated. Some lacked hands, some feet, some ears and noses. They were men who had learned skills and crafts and done well in training; after which their other extremities had been cut off and they were left only with those on which their work depended."

Alexander wept for them. He offered them money and safe return to Greece, but they replied that they had no wish to be oddities in their homeland. Instead, they asked for land where they could live on their own. Alexander gave them land, money, clothing, seeds, and livestock.

If this story of mutilated slaves is true, it may be the reason Alexander allowed his men to sack the city. In Babylon and Susa, he had controlled them, but in Persepolis he did not. The soldiers streamed through the city, taking women, jewels, money—anything they saw was fair game.

Alexander himself saw to the treasury. The man who had been in charge of it had kept it safe in the terrible panic before Alexander marched into the city. He had done Alexander a great service, for the treasury contained three times what the one at Susa had held.

The Greeks celebrated. Their task, as put forth by the League of Corinth six years earlier, was finished. They had freed the Greek cities in Asia and avenged the Persian invasion of Greece. The Palace of Xerxes, the magnificent building that was the center of Persepolis, was burned to the ground to avenge the long-ago burning of Athens.

There is a legend, probably untrue, that a lady named Thais (below) suggested to Alexander that he burn Persepolis.

Chapter 7
Rigorous Days and
Persian Ways

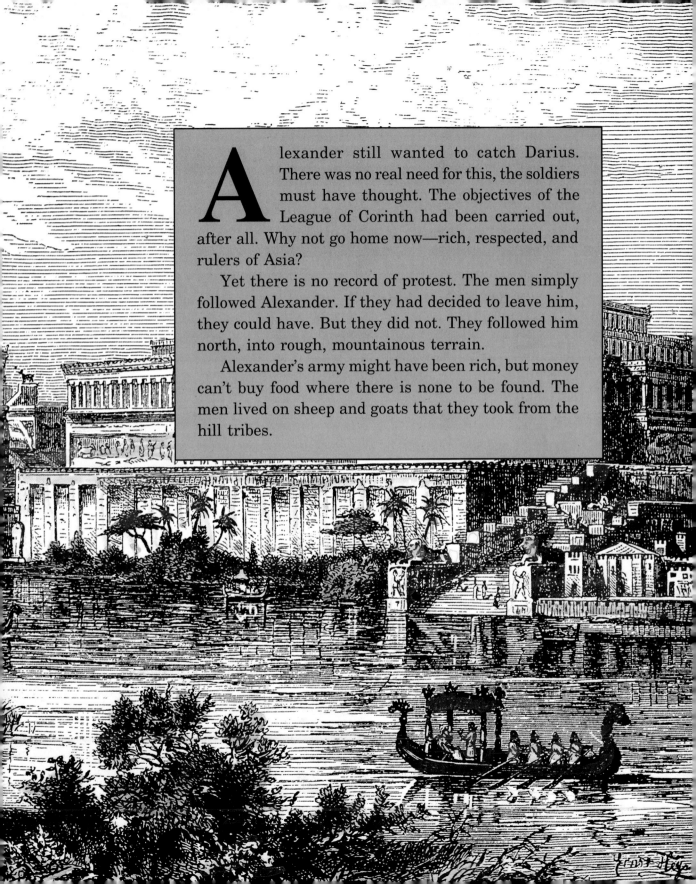

Alexander still wanted to catch Darius. There was no real need for this, the soldiers must have thought. The objectives of the League of Corinth had been carried out, after all. Why not go home now—rich, respected, and rulers of Asia?

Yet there is no record of protest. The men simply followed Alexander. If they had decided to leave him, they could have. But they did not. They followed him north, into rough, mountainous terrain.

Alexander's army might have been rich, but money can't buy food where there is none to be found. The men lived on sheep and goats that they took from the hill tribes.

At a place called Ecbatana (now Hamadan, Iran), Alexander released his Greek allies from service in his army. They were welcome to enlist again, and many did. Those who went home went with farewell gifts.

From Ecbatana, Alexander and a few swift forces galloped eastward in pursuit of Darius. The Persian king was known to have retreated to the province of Bactria, hundreds of miles to the east in what is now Afghanistan. Many horses died of heat exhaustion in the chase. After two days, far short of Bactria, Darius was found, stabbed to death, in a wagon. Alexander took off his cloak and wrapped his former enemy in it. He sent the corpse to Persepolis for a royal burial.

Alexander waited for the rest of his men to catch up with him at a place they called Hecatompylos, "city of a hundred gates," because it was situated at a crossroads. There, once the men were all together, Alexander spoke to them about what lay ahead. He hoped to inspire them with his own ambition for further conquests. The men are said to have remained silent after the speech, until a soldier shouted, "Lead us, lead us wherever you will!" And the rest of the men joined in.

Alexander was still loved and trusted by his men. That trust, however, was soon to waver.

Alexander began to wear Persian clothing. He didn't adopt Persian dress completely. It is believed that he simply added a few Persian accessories to his usual Macedonian clothes. But it was enough to cause unrest among some of his men. They were Greeks and had long been taught that Greek customs and dress were superior to all others, as the Greek people were superior.

Alexander discovering the body of Darius

There was yet another fly in the ointment. Alexander believed that superior people were to be found in all races of men. He now began to allow a few Persians the same privileges and positions that had been reserved for Greeks, especially Macedonians.

Alexander busied himself planning his next campaign and managing the business of his empire and his army. But people always wanted to see him, and there was usually a line outside his tent. Macedonians felt that they should not have to wait behind Persians. But Alexander treated all his men alike.

Alexander continued on his eastward march, inspiring loyalty mixed with fear. One of Alexander's officers, a man named Philotas, was very popular with the soldiers. Alexander learned that Philotas had been warned of a plot to kill the king, but that Philotas had not told him. Alexander had Philotas arrested and tried before the Macedonian Assembly, his elite group of voting soldiers. Philotas was found guilty of treason and put to death.

Macedonian law also allowed the king to kill anyone related to a traitor. Unfortunately, Philotas was the son of Parmenio, Alexander's second-in-command, who had fought so well and worked so hard for the king. Alexander had Parmenio killed, too. If there was little grumbling about this, it may have been because the men were afraid.

The man responsible for the murder of Darius was called Bessus. He was still in control of parts of the old Persian empire. Alexander learned that Bessus had declared himself Darius's successor and was gathering an army in the province of Bactria.

To engage Bessus in battle, Alexander would have to cross the unbelievably high, rough Hindu Kush mountain range. To surprise Bessus, Alexander would cross these mountains in the early spring, while they were still packed with ice and snow. And to cross the Hindu Kush, Alexander needed a smaller, lighter army. He left half his men behind to establish cities, govern them, and beat down any rebellions.

The remaining men climbed with Alexander. The air grew thinner. They were far, still, from their true test. These were merely foothills. There was a period of rest, over winter, and then in May the army started up the south face of the Hindu Kush.

Crevasses and steep walls of rock make for a difficult entry into Afghanistan.

They climbed 11,650 feet (over 2 miles; 3,550 meters) on short supplies. It took a week to get up and ten days to get down. Many horses and mules starved. The men themselves, close to freezing and starving, ate the animals raw. Alexander was as cold and hungry as any of the men.

From the terrible cold, the army came down into terrible heat. They were weak and tired. Bessus could easily have beaten them. But Bessus had heard that Alexander led the army. The very name caused dread. What kind of man could lead an army over the mountains in the snow and ice? Afraid to meet Alexander, Bessus and his men fled across the Oxus River (now the Amu Darya) and burned their boats.

Alexander did as he had years before. He had the hide tents stuffed with straw and made into rafts. Bessus was captured, stripped, and whipped. He was sent back to Ecbatana to be punished and executed.

Alexander had treated Darius with honor, wrapping the man's body in his own cloak and sending it for a royal funeral. This was because Darius had been a king, and Alexander saw himself as the king's heir. Alexander treated Bessus as a criminal because he had been a traitor to Darius and had never, therefore, been a true king.

Alexander and his army moved north toward the river Jaxartes, today's Syr Darya in the Soviet Union. The Jaxartes marked the northernmost reaches of the Persian empire. There they raided tribes in the river valleys for food. Alexander was shot in the leg with an arrow in one of the raids, and he had to be carried along on a stretcher. The soldiers quarreled about who would have the honor of carrying him.

That winter, twenty-three thousand replacement troops arrived. Four thousand animals had been hunted, killed, and salted down for the army's future marches. The whole army looked forward to the spring.

But in the spring of 328 B.C., Alexander, in a drunken rage, killed one of his officers, Cleitus, who had saved his life at the Granicus River years before. Cleitus had insulted Alexander at a drinking party and refused to back down. The king snatched a spear from a guard and ran it through Cleitus.

There is nothing in the record of Alexander's life that shows him to be more ashamed of himself than he was over this. He stopped eating and stayed in his tent. His men grew so worried about him that they decreed that Cleitus had been guilty of treason and so

Alexander and his men crossing the Jaxartes River

Alexander in despair after killing Cleitus

deserved to die. But the men close to Alexander, his officers, saw that danger lay in opposing the king. From then on they would play it safe.

There was yet another thorny issue that arose between Alexander and his men. The Macedonian soldiers were disgusted by the Persian custom of *proskynesis*—bowing deeply and even lying face-down on the ground before a king. Macedonians' tradition held that kings were men as they were. They would serve and honor their king, of course, but they could also remove him from office if he displeased them. They would not bow to their king.

While the Macedonians looked down on the Persians for performing the *proskynesis*, the Persians resented the Macedonians for *not* doing it. Alexander began to like the Persian custom and asked the Macedonians to begin at least bowing when they saw him. His old soldiers indignantly refused. Alexander understood that he was asking too much and found a graceful way to back down. But some damage had been done to their feeling for him.

Alexander recovered from his leg wound and led his men north into Sogdia, now a part of the Soviet Union. There they found a tribe of people who had taken refuge on top of a high rock. There was no way but one, it seemed, to scale its sheer face, and the one way up was well defended.

Alexander offered a treaty with the two tribesmen who had climbed down to meet with him. They laughed and told him that the Macedonians would have to buy wings even to meet them in battle. It was their big mistake.

Determined to beat them, Alexander offered huge rewards to the expert climbers among his men. Three hundred volunteered. That night, in the snow, the men scaled the steepest unguarded side of the rock. In the morning the people of the tribe were shocked to see the Macedonian soldiers and surrendered. There was a feast then, and women dancers performed for Alexander and his officers. The king fell in love with one of the women, Roxane, who was the daughter of the chief Oxyartes. They were married soon after that.

The Macedonian soldiers were unhappy with the marriage. They felt that Alexander should have married a Greek, preferably a Macedonian. Anyone else was a barbarian.

Probably no one but Alexander's closest friend, Hephaestion, shared his belief that men should be judged on merit, not race. It baffled Alexander's men that he wanted to wear Persian-style clothing and to appoint men of the lands he had conquered to important positions in his court and army. The soldiers didn't understand that Alexander foresaw an empire in which ideas flowed freely as the spices and cloths of regular trade. An empire built on the strengths of its many cultures, he believed, would be stronger than an empire with one culture forced upon it.

In fact, soon after the wedding, Alexander recruited thirty thousand boys from Persian villages. They would be brought up in the Greek way. Once they had learned to speak Greek, they could fight in his army. His soldiers were not pleased.

Alexander persuading his men to continue east and invade India after his conquest of the Persian Empire

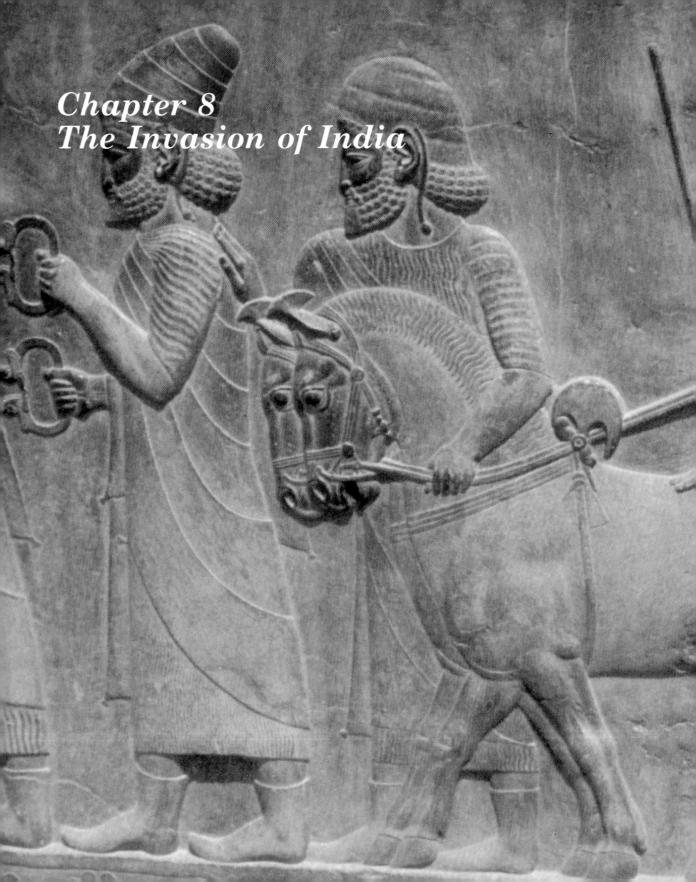

Chapter 8
The Invasion of India

Alexander now planned an invasion of India. All his planning, however, couldn't cancel out the fact that the maps of his time were incorrect. India was really twice as big as Alexander thought. And he had no idea—no one did at that time—how truly huge the continent of Asia is. He had marched his men beyond what any of his maps showed.

Alexander planned to march to the Outer Ocean, an ocean the Greeks thought lay at the end of the world, in just a few months. To that end, in 327 B.C., he gathered the largest force of his career: 120,000 men from all over his new empire. He encouraged his men to travel light, and he burned his wagon of possessions as an example. After many of his men had followed suit, they marched on toward India.

Alexander had many battles in India, but two are especially impressive. One was the attack on a band of rebels on a lofty plateau called Pir-Sar, high above the Indus River Valley.

The rebels could not be starved out—there was plenty of good land for growing crops atop their stronghold. It was surrounded by gorges and ravines. One ravine was 800 feet (244 meters) deep. Alexander ordered that a bridge be built across it. Once the bridge was built, he and thirty companions crossed and began climbing Pir-Sar. The rebels rolled boulders down on them, killing all but Alexander. Three nights later, Alexander climbed up a rope and led his men in a victorious attack on the rebels.

Alexander's last great battle was against the Indian king Porus. The Hydaspes River (now called the Jhelum) divided the two great armies. Porus had more men than Alexander, and he had two hundred elephants, too. Alexander saw that crossing the river on horses straight into the elephants wouldn't work. He had to think of a plan.

It was the monsoon season. It rained constantly. In the rain, Alexander had his troops prepare for battle over and over. Porus and his men watched them for days, reacting every time any soldiers set out in boats as if to cross the river. Alexander also acted as if he meant to stay camped for a long time. He had wagonloads of food carted into camp.

Porus didn't know what to think or expect, and after a while, he began not to care. When Porus quit reacting to Alexander's movements, Alexander knew it was time to move.

The army rafted across the river in the dead of night. Porus, acting too late, sent chariots and horse-

Alexander's troops battling King Porus at the Hydaspes River

men. The fighting lasted for hours in the pouring rain. Porus and his men were brave and fought well. Finally, Alexander and his men succeeded in causing a panic among the elephants. The great beasts began trampling Porus's soldiers and retreating. Porus surrendered soon after that.

Porus was a tall and dignified man. Alexander asked him how he wished to be treated. "As a king," answered Porus.

"I would do that for my own sake," said Alexander. "Ask for yours."

Porus's surrender to Alexander

Porus simply repeated what he had said before. Alexander restored Porus's kingdom, making it even larger than before. He even honored Porus's elephant by dedicating to it a temple in the city of Taxila, where the great animal lived to an old age.

Around the time of the battle against Porus, Alexander's horse Bucephalus died. The king grieved for days. The ancient historian Arrian wrote:

"In the plains where the battle was fought, and which he set out from to cross the Hydaspes, Alexander founded cities. The first he called Nicaea, from his victory over the Indians; the other Bucephala, in memory of his horse Bucephalus, who died there, not wounded at all but from exhaustion and old age. For he was about thirty years old and fell victim to fa-

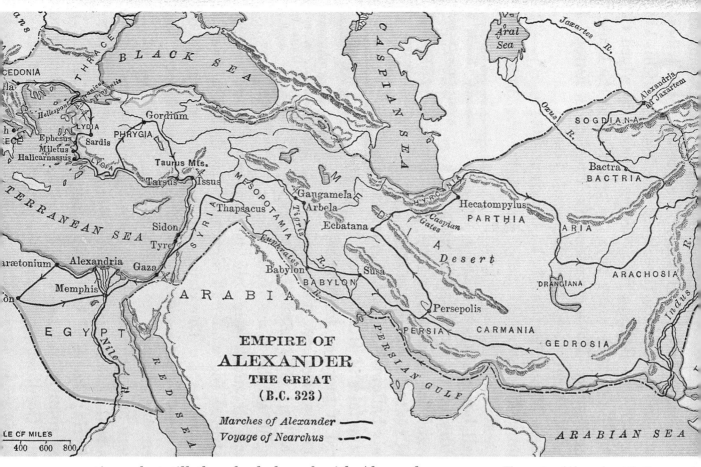

Empire of Alexander the Great (B.C. 323) map showing territories including Macedonia, Thrace, Black Sea, Caspian Sea, Sogdiana, Bactria, Mediterranean Sea, Egypt, Arabia, Babylon, Persia, Gedrosia, Arachosia, and the Arabian Sea.

EMPIRE OF ALEXANDER THE GREAT (B.C. 323)

Marches of Alexander ———
Voyage of Nearchus ·—·—

SCALE OF MILES
400   600   800

The empire of Alexander at the time of his death. Afghanistan (Bactria) and India are on the right of the map.

tigue; but till then had shared with Alexander many labors and dangers, never mounted except by him, since Bucephalus would bear no other rider. He was tall in stature, and valiant of heart."

After the battle against Porus, Alexander's soldiers became more restless. They had been away from their homes for eight years. There was no end in sight to this campaign of Alexander's, and it seemed pointless. He was by far the richest man in the world. The soldiers were mostly men in their fifties and sixties. They all had enough money and loot to live well back in Macedon and Greece. They wanted to go home. One of their generals, Coenus, spoke up for them. They were weary and homesick. They wanted to see their wives and children. Let them go home.

Alexander sulked like a child, but his men would not give in. After three days, Alexander did. They would return home. But they would follow the route that he chose. He said they must allow him to leave India in dignity, not run from it.

First they built a fleet of ships that would sail down the Indus River toward the Arabian Sea. Along the banks marched the soldiers, fighting local tribes all the way. In one battle, Alexander leaped onto the city wall, then jumped down among the enemy. Before he could be assisted, he had been badly wounded in the chest. An arrow ripped through his chest wall, and his lung collapsed. He continued to fight after

Alexander's surgeon trying to remove the arrow lodged in his side

receiving the wound but eventually lost consciousness. His soldiers thought he was dead and fought hysterically, killing everyone in the city.

After the battle, Alexander was kept at a camp ten miles (sixteen kilometers) by river from the army's base camp. Even as he began to recover, the men at the base camp became more and more convinced that he was dead and that the generals were hiding the truth from them. When Alexander realized this, even though his wound was still only a week old, he had himself carried to a ship on the river. He wanted to reassure his men that he was still alive. One of his admirals, Nearchus, wrote about the scene:

"As soon as the ship bearing the King began to near the camp, he ordered the awning to be furled from the stern, so that all could see him. Even then the men doubted, thinking Alexander's corpse was being brought there; till at last, when the ship had moored, he raised his hand to the crowd; and they cried aloud, some holding up their hands to heaven, some towards Alexander; and uncontrollable tears were shed in their astonished joy. Some of the bodyguards brought him a litter as he was being carried off the ship; but he ordered a horse to be fetched him. And when he mounted it, and everyone saw him, the whole army clapped their hands repeatedly, and the banks and river-glades threw back the sound. Then when Alexander was near his tent he got off his horse, so that the army could see him walking. They all ran to him from every side, some touching his hands, some his knees, some his clothing; others just looked from nearby and blessed him as he went; some threw garlands on him, of whatever Indian flowers were then in bloom."

The wound eventually healed, but the fractured ribs and torn flesh and muscle must have fused to make one huge mass of scar tissue. Every breath he took must have hurt him for the rest of his life. And this wound is certainly a reason the rest of his life was so short.

After recovering enough to travel again, Alexander led his men on an 1,100-mile (1,770-kilometer) trek through the desert of Gedrosia, alongside the Arabian Sea. He planned the march carefully, knowing what a toll the desert could exact. His fleet was to sail beside the troops, carrying food and fodder for the animals in special flat-bottomed Indian boats.

Weather and an Indian uprising caused delays for the fleet. Alexander and his troops struggled through the deep sand, trying to avoid poisonous snakes and always, always, thinking of water.

When they did come upon water, some of the men dived into it and drank till they died. Alexander learned to avoid this problem by camping a mile or more from the water supply and having it carried to camp. One terrible night they camped in a dry river bed. It rained, and a flash flood swept away people, animals, tents, and weapons.

The march was worse than all the other hardships they'd endured put together. Alexander held the army together by example. He forbade any officers to ride, and he himself refused to ride a horse. A tired, thirsty soldier could see his king staggering, just as tired and thirsty, through the sand. In fact, when some scouts found enough water to fill a helmet and brought it to Alexander, he thanked them and poured it out onto the sand. He would not drink while his men were thirsty.

At the end of the march, as the men who had survived it regained their strength, Alexander dealt with problems that had come up while he was in the north and east.

Many of the leaders Alexander had left in charge of conquered lands had believed he would never return. They had used their power to become rich at the expense of their subjects. Alexander was quick to put these men on trial and punish them, Persians and Macedonians alike.

Portrait of Alexander astride his horse Bucephalus

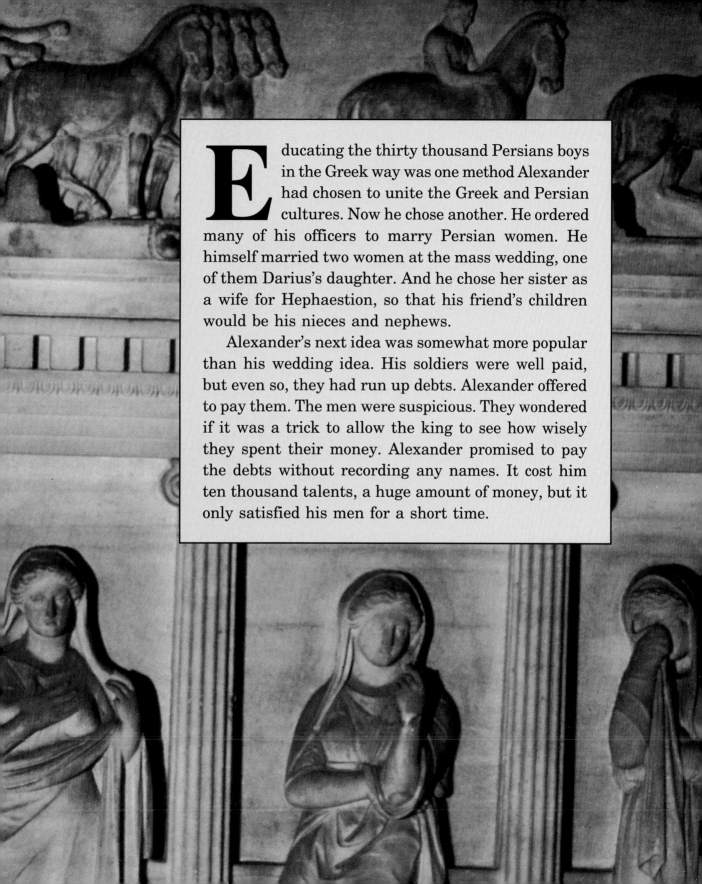

Educating the thirty thousand Persians boys in the Greek way was one method Alexander had chosen to unite the Greek and Persian cultures. Now he chose another. He ordered many of his officers to marry Persian women. He himself married two women at the mass wedding, one of them Darius's daughter. And he chose her sister as a wife for Hephaestion, so that his friend's children would be his nieces and nephews.

Alexander's next idea was somewhat more popular than his wedding idea. His soldiers were well paid, but even so, they had run up debts. Alexander offered to pay them. The men were suspicious. They wondered if it was a trick to allow the king to see how wisely they spent their money. Alexander promised to pay the debts without recording any names. It cost him ten thousand talents, a huge amount of money, but it only satisfied his men for a short time.

Construction of a palace under the direction of Alexander

The thirty thousand Persian boys were eighteen years old now. They were brought to Susa, where Alexander was staying, to be displayed to the king. They handled their Macedonian weapons with skill and looked handsome and graceful in their Macedonian clothing.

Alexander was well pleased, but his old Macedonian soldiers were furious. When Alexander announced his plan to discharge his oldest soldiers—with large bonuses, of course—they felt insulted. It was one thing to march home all together, a victorious army. It was another to be replaced, and by barbarians at that.

He'd made the announcement expecting to be cheered. Instead, the men shouted at him. Alexander jumped down among them. He quieted them and then got up before them again. He reminded them that they had been meek shepherds back in Macedon. Now they ruled the world. He defied them to name a single man who had been killed in retreat as long as he had led them. He threatened to replace the whole army with Persians.

The men asked his forgiveness. Alexander let them worry for days, then forgave them by calling them his kinsmen and letting them kiss him. A huge feast was held, and then ten thousand old soldiers left for Macedon with honors.

The court of Alexander, from a fif-teenth-century manuscript

Alexander mourning the death of Hephaestion

Soon after this, Hephaestion, Alexander's best friend, died. The king clung for a day and a night to the body. He mourned wildly, cut off all his hair, ordered the manes and tails of his horses cut short, and hanged Hephaestion's doctor. He ordered tributes to Hephaestion throughout his empire. And he sent to the priests at Siwah in Egypt, asking them to declare that Hephaestion had been a god.

Alexander had always found relief in action, so now he led a force into the hills against a tribe that had been causing problems. After subduing them, he went to Babylon. He was planning a campaign to the west. He would explore North Africa and construct a road to the Strait of Gibraltar. In the meantime, he

Alexander, mortally ill, meeting with his faithful officers

worried about irrigation on the Euphrates River—how could he improve it for the farmers downstream? And he planned a new city.

Alexander got a fever in June of 323 B.C. There is some suspicion that he was poisoned, but any number of things could have made him ill. Little was known then about what actually caused and spread disease. Even the water at that time could kill a man. Alexander had been boating near a marsh and might have caught malaria from the bite of a mosquito. At any rate, he developed pneumonia and was near death when his soldiers demanded to see him. They filed past, the thousands of men, and Alexander managed to raise a hand or nod or make eye contact with each of them.

As he drew closer to death, the story goes, his generals asked him, "To whom do you leave your kingdom?"

Alexander struggled to form the words: "To the strongest." And when he was asked at what time he wanted his divine honors paid him, he is said to have replied, "When you are happy." Those were his last words. He died on June 13, 323 B.C.

There was such chaos after Alexander's death that his body was left in his tent for hours in the heat. According to accounts, however, the body did not begin to decay. Some said it was because the life force in Alexander was so strong that it left him more slowly than it would leave an ordinary man. Today we know it is more likely that Alexander slipped into a deep coma and seemed dead for a few hours before he really died.

The death of Alexander

His generals burst into the tent at one point and fought about how they would honor him and who would take charge. Finally the embalmers came. They prayed that it would be right for them to handle the body of a god, then set to work.

His vital organs were removed, his body steeped in preservative and then embedded in precious spices such as myrrh. He was finally covered in gold leaf.

As the body was prepared, his generals and men saw to it that Alexander would have the most expensive, ornate, and beautiful funeral procession ever imagined. Greek craftsmen worked for two years on the funeral car that would bear Alexander's body from Babylon to his own city of Alexandria in Egypt.

Alexander's wife Roxane weeping over his body: a Persian painting of the early fourteenth century

("Leaf from a Shahnamah: The Bier of Iskandar [Alexander the Great]"; Mongol period, Tabriz school, color and gold: 25.0 x 28.0 cm [9 13/16 x 11 in.])

111

The body lay in its bed of spices in a gold casket, which was covered with a richly embroidered purple cloth. The funeral car was made to resemble a small, golden temple. Its entrance was guarded by golden lions. Gold columns held up a roof of gold and jewels. An olive wreath, the Greek symbol of victory, had been made from beaten gold, and it rose above the roof, flashing in the sunshine. Statues of the Greek god Victory stood at each corner of the roof. Under the peaks of the roof there were paintings of Alexander and his army. Between the columns, the open spaces were draped with golden net.

The wheels of the funeral car were painted with gold. At the hub of each wheel was a golden head of a lion, a spear held in its teeth. The car was drawn by sixty-four mules, each wearing a crown, gold bells, and a gem-studded collar.

The craftsmen also fitted the funeral car with shock absorbers, though no one today is sure how that was done. The body was to be carefully protected on its long journey. For all the thousand-mile trip, road makers went before the procession to smooth the way for Alexander's body.

Alexander's friend and general, Ptolemy, had been left behind to govern Egypt. He rode with his army to Syria to meet the funeral procession and brought the body to its final resting place. Ptolemy ordered a tomb built in Alexandria for his friend, commander, and king.

As the magnificent funeral car, with its massive honor guard, was drawn across Asia, thousands of people came out to see it and to pay homage to Alexander. Children asked questions, adults answered with stories. This is probably how many of the legends

Alexander's funeral procession

of Alexander began. They would not have lasted long, however, had his life not been truly marvelous in the first place.

What did Alexander mean when he said, "To the strongest"? No one knows now, and certainly no one knew then, though several men said they did.

Two of Alexander's wives were pregnant. He may have meant that the Macedonian Assembly should choose between the two children, if they both were males, when the time came. Or he may simply have meant that the man who *could* rule his kingdom *should* rule his kingdom. In death, as he had in life, he might have been challenging his men. Or he may not have said it at all. It may only be another of the stories that were told and have lived through the ages about this amazing man.

In the end, no one proved as strong as Alexander had been. He'd used the force of his personality to hold his empire together. Without him, it split into several separate kingdoms. Those lands remained under Greek or Macedonian influence for the next two hundred years.

Alexander's name alone caused dread in those who wished to oppose him. The sight of him inspired ordinary soldiers to acts of courage they hadn't dreamed they were capable of.

His open mind had seen opportunities where other men saw problems. His intelligence, courage, and tenacity made him one of the world's truly great military leaders.

Map showing the various kingdoms into which Alexander's empire had split by 301 B.C., twenty-two years after his death

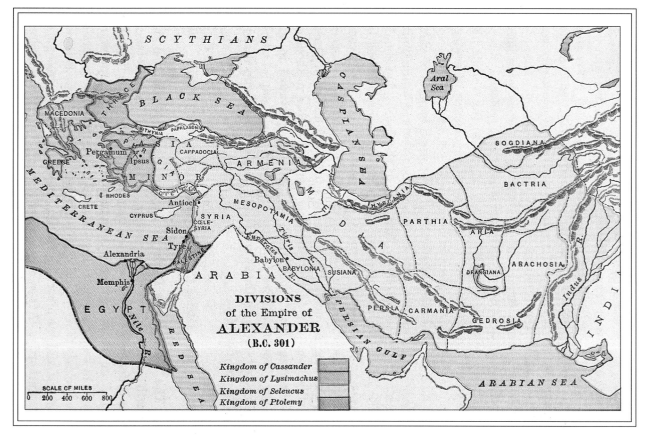

DIVISIONS
of the Empire of
ALEXANDER
(B.C. 301)

Kingdom of Cassander
Kingdom of Lysimachus
Kingdom of Seleucus
Kingdom of Ptolemy

SCALE OF MILES
0   200   400   600   800

He had been cruel in a time when cruelty was a common, accepted way of life. But he had shown compassion when it was seen not as a virtue but as the refuge of a weakling.

He was merciless to his enemies, but the rare, high love that is friendship was so basic to him that he risked his life to keep it. The death of a friend, whether it was a dog, a horse, or a man, could drive him nearly mad with grief.

Alexander wanted honor and glory and got both, but getting them only made him want more. He left an army, which eventually disbanded; an empire, which broke apart; and his name, Alexander, which has captivated mankind for over two thousand years.

Head of Alexander the Great, by the Greek sculptor Lysippus

Appendices

Alexander invaded Asia with about 43,000 infantry, or foot soldiers, and 6,000 cavalry, or horsemen. Greek warriors (left) carried both spears and short swords. On the back of the shield was a strap by which to hold it and a metal strip that ran across the forearm. Armor was reinforced with leather to protect the body. Some men wore metal breastplates for protection.

Philip, Alexander's father, had redesigned the spears, called sarissas, to a length of sixteen feet (almost five meters). It usually took two hands to hold one. As the spear-bearers advanced into battle, they waved their sarissas up and down rhythmically. This frightened and confused the enemy.

Horsemen rode without stirrups or saddles. When their arms were occupied in combat, they guided their horses with their knees.

Alexander the Great founded the city of Alexandria, Egypt, in 332 B.C. After his death, when the Ptolemies ruled Egypt, the city grew to be an exciting center of culture, learning, and trade. Greek and Hebrew scholars and intellectuals found in Alexandria a place to study and to share their knowledge with one another.

The Alexandrian Library (left), founded by Ptolemy I and expanded by Ptolemy II, grew to be the largest collection of writings in the ancient world. The library and its museum housed more than 500,000 volumes. They included the Greek manuscript of the Bible, maps and star charts, and Persian, Jewish, Greek, Latin, and Egyptian literature. The library burned when Julius Caesar attacked the city in 48 B.C. In A.D. 391, the Roman emperor Theodosius ordered all of Alexandria's temples to be burned, and in the process, the museum was destroyed, too.

Today in Egypt, plans are underway to make Alexandria once again a great center of learning. The Egyptian government and the United Nations Educational, Social, and Cultural Organization (UNESCO) are working to rebuild the Alexandrian Library. The new complex will include a four-million-volume library, a planetarium, a science museum, and other study centers.

Timeline of Events in Alexander's Lifetime

All dates are B.C.

356—Alexander is born in Pella, capital of Madecon, to Philip II and his wife Olympias of Epirus

343–340—The Greek philosopher Aristotle tutors Alexander

340—Alexander subdues a rebellion of tribes in Illyrium

338—In charge of the cavalry, Alexander aids his father in defeating the Greek city-states

337—Philip divorces Olympias and marries a Macedonian woman; he and Alexander quarrel at the wedding and Philip sends Alexander into exile

336—Philip is murdered, and army commanders proclaim Alexander king of Macedon

335—Alexander leads his army across the Ister (Danube) River and defeats the Getae; he returns to the Greek peninsula to put down a revolt in Thebes and destroys the city

334—Alexander crosses the Dardanelles and begins his invasion of the Persian Empire; he fights his first battle with King Darius's army at the Granicus River

333—At Gordium in Phrygia, Alexander cuts the famous Gordian Knot; his army defeats Darius's troops at the Battle of Issus; Darius flees, leaving his wife and mother behind with Alexander

332—After a seven-month siege, Alexander's army defeats the city of Tyre and takes control of the east coast of the Mediterranean; Alexander marches into Egypt, is crowned a pharoah, consults the oracle at Siwah, and founds the city of Alexandria

331—Alexander leaves Egypt and marches toward Mesopotamia; his troops defeat Darius's Persians at Gaugamela; Alexander occupies the Persian cities of Babylon, Susa, and Persepolis

330—On the road to Persia's eastern provinces, Alexander discovers the body of Darius, who had been murdered by Bessus, the Persian governor of Bactria (Afghanistan)

329—Alexander crosses the Hindu Kush mountain range, carrying his military campaign into the far northeastern reaches of the Persian Empire

328—In a drunken rage, Alexander kills his officer Cleitus

327—Recrossing the Hindu Kush, Alexander embarks on his invasion of India

326—Alexander defeats Porus at the Hydaspes River; Alexander's beloved horse Bucephalus dies, and he names a city Bucephala in its honor

325—Alexander begins his return trip across the mountains and deserts of Gedrosia; his admiral Nearchus, meanwhile, voyages along the coast

324—As part of his policy to merge Greek and Persian cultures, Alexander has eighty of his Macedonian officers marry Persian women; he takes 30,000 Persian young men into his army and sends Macedonian veterans home

323—Alexander dies in Babylon on June 13

Glossary of Terms

barbarian—A person thought to be uncivilized and uncultured

battering ram—A war machine with an iron head on a long beam, used to batter holes in walls

catapult—A military device for hurling stones or other objects toward the enemy

causeway—A raised roadway across water

cavalry, cavalrymen—Horsemen; soldiers on horseback

city-state—A city and the territory around it, functioning together as a unit of government

coma—An unconscious state due to injury or disease

cornel—A family of flowering hardwood trees or shrubs that includes the dogwood

fly in the ointment—Something that worsens or spoils a situation

infantry, infantrymen—Foot soldiers

invincible—Unable to be conquered

lime—A white-powdered calcium compound used in building construction, farming, and many other areas

lyre—A harp-like musical instrument

marathon—A long-distance foot race, named for a runner's sprint from Marathon to Athens in 490 B.C. to announce the Greek victory over the Persians

monsoon—Severe, seasonal winds and rains in southern Asia

omen—A hint or sign of things to come

oracle—A priest or priestess who was believed to obtain information or predictions from a god

phalanx—In ancient Greek warfare, a block of foot soldiers eight rows deep

potion—A liquid medicine

prophecy—A prediction about future events

sarissa—A Macedonian spear of cornel wood, 16 feet (4.9 meters) long

satrap—Governor of a Persian province

scimitar—A large sword with a curved blade

seer—A person who has deep insights or predicts events

siege tower—A tower from which an army carries on a prolonged attack

talent—An ancient Greek unit of money, equal to 6,000 drachmas

Bibliography

For further reading, see:

Fox, Robin Lane. *The Search for Alexander*. Boston: Little, Brown and Company, 1980.

Krensky, Stephen. *Conqueror and Hero*. Boston: Little, Brown and Company, 1980.

Mercer, Charles, and the editors of Horizon Magazine. *Alexander the Great*. NY: American Heritage Publishing Co., 1962.

Renault, Mary. *The Nature of Alexander*. NY: Pantheon Books, 1975.

Renault, Mary. *The Persian Boy*. NY: Random House, 1972. (Fiction)

Robinson, Charles Alexander. *Alexander the Great: Conqueror and Creator of a New World*. NY: Franklin Watts, 1963.

Index

Page numbers in boldface type indicate illustrations.

Picture Identifications for Chapter Opening Spreads

6-7—Mosaic of Alexander the Great from Pompeii, in the National Archaeological Museum, Naples, Italy
12-13—Cape Sounion, Greece
30-31—The Acropolis, Parthenon, and other ancient structures in Athens, Greece
38-39—Lion attacking a horse in a bas relief in Persepolis
50-51—The remains of the Persian city of Persepolis
66-67—The pyramids of Giza, Egypt
84-85—The Assyrian royal palace at Nineveh
94-95—Ancient Persian chariot, in a bas relief from Persepolis, now in the British Museum
104-105—Mourners on a Greek-style sarcophagus from Sidon

Acknowledgment

For a critical reading of the manuscript, our thanks to John Parker, Ph.D., Curator, James Ford Bell Library, University of Minnesota, Minneapolis, Minnesota

Picture Acknowledgments

The Bettmann Archive—8, 9, 29, 32, 52, 71, 75, 91, 100, 108, 110, 113, 115

Bridgeman Art Library/SuperStock—93, 106, 107

Courtesy of the Freer Gallery of Art, Smithsonian Institution, Washington, D.C., accession no. 38.3—111

© **Virginia Grimes**—48

Historical Pictures Service, Chicago—2, 23, 24 (margin), 34, 41, 43, 49, 60, 64, 69, 70, 72, 87, 90, 97, 103, 109

© **Museum of Fine Arts**, Boston—4

North Wind Picture Archives—10, 11, 15, 17, 22, 25, 27, 35, 36, 37, 42, 44, 45, 46, 47, 53, 57, 58, 59, 61, 62, 77, 79, 83, 84-85, 89, 99, 114, 116, 118

Courtesy of The Oriental Institute of the University of Chicago—81

Odyssey Productions: © Robert Frerck—5, 6-7, 12-13, 18, 21, 30-31, 66-67, 104-105

Root Resources: © Jane P. Downton—94-95; © Irene E. Hubbell—38-39, 50-51

H. Armstrong Roberts—16, 68, 78, 98

Tony Stone Worldwide/Chicago, Ltd.: © Don Smetzer—82; © Bill Staley—63

SuperStock—20, 24 (top), 54, 55, 65, 73

About the Author

Maureen Ash grew up reading books in Milaca, Minnesota. She and her husband raise and work Norwegian Fjord and Suffolk draft horses. They enjoy running, rollerblading, their two small children, and Roy, the family cat.